PRAISE FOR

PRAYING WITH AUTHORITY

Praying with Authority is a clear, concise and practical guide for all
of us who believe in the power of prayer. It is packed with personal
experiences and couched within a strong biblical framework.

TED HAGGARD
SENIOR PASTOR, NEW LIFE CHURCH
COLORADO SPRINGS, COLORADO

The Body of Christ stands at an incredible crossroads.
At these crossroads also stands the plan of the enemy to stop God's
kingdom from moving forward. But God—He gives His people
authority to open up the way ahead! If ever there is a book needed at
this time, it is *Praying with Authority*. The prayer movement makes its
shift this decade from supplication to declaration and proclamation.
Read this book and it will help you make the shift into supernatural
praying and change the atmosphere and society where you live.

CHUCK D. PIERCE
VICE PRESIDENT, GLOBAL HARVEST MINISTRIES
PRESIDENT, GLORY OF ZION INTERNATIONAL MINISTRIES, INC.
DENTON, TEXAS

To teach about authority one must know what authority
is and have experience operating in it. Barbara Wentroble qualifies on
both levels. This is why she was able to write *Praying with Authority*
with such effectiveness. Her dynamic teaching style will lift us to
more effective prayer—to see God's kingdom come to Earth.

DUTCH SHEETS
AUTHOR, *INTERCESSORY PRAYER*
COLORADO SPRINGS, COLORADO

I love Barbara! She is a no-nonsense kind of writer.
In *Praying with Authority* she gives practical information for everyone,
regardless if one is a beginner or a seasoned intercessor.
Her stories are great too! Read it.

ALICE SMITH
EXECUTIVE DIRECTOR, U.S. PRAYER CENTER
HOUSTON, TEXAS

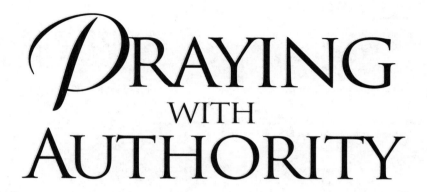

PRAYING
WITH
AUTHORITY

BARBARA
WENTROBLE

Regal

From Gospel Light
Ventura, California, U.S.A.

PUBLISHED BY REGAL BOOKS
FROM GOSPEL LIGHT
VENTURA, CALIFORNIA, U.S.A.
PRINTED IN THE U.S.A.

Regal

Regal Books is a ministry of Gospel Light, a Christian publisher dedicated to serving the local church. We believe God's vision for Gospel Light is to provide church leaders with biblical, user-friendly materials that will help them evangelize, disciple and minister to children, youth and families.

It is our prayer that this Regal book will help you discover biblical truth for your own life and help you meet the needs of others. May God richly bless you.

For a free catalog of resources from Regal Books/Gospel Light, please call your Christian supplier or contact us at 1-800-4-GOSPEL or www.regalbooks.com.

All Scripture quotations, unless otherwise indicated, are taken from the NEW AMERI-CAN STANDARD BIBLE®, Copyright © 1960, 1962, 1963, 1968, 1971, 1972, 1973, 1975, 1977, 1995 by The Lockman Foundation. Used by permission.

The other versions used are
AMP–Scripture taken from *THE AMPLIFIED BIBLE*, Old Testament copyright © 1965, 1987 by the Zondervan Corporation. The Amplified New Testament copyright © 1958, 1987 by The Lockman Foundation. Used by permission.
KJV–*King James Version.* Authorized King James Version.

Cover and interior design by Robert Williams
Edited by Kathi Macias

Library of Congress Cataloging-in-Publication Data
Wentroble, Barbara, 1943–
    Praying with authority / Barbara Wentroble.
        p. cm.
Includes bibliographical references.
    ISBN 0-8307-3129-6
    1. Prayer—Christianity. I. Title.
    BV210.3.W46 2003
    248.3'2—dc21   2003001591

2 3 4 5 6 7 8 9 10 11 12 13 14 15 / 15 14 13 12 11 10 09 08 07 06 05

Rights for publishing this book in other languages are contracted by Gospel Light World-wide, the international nonprofit ministry of Gospel Light. Gospel Light Worldwide also provides publishing and technical assistance to international publishers dedicated to producing Sunday School and Vacation Bible School curricula and books in the lan-guages of the world. For additional information, visit www.gospellightworldwide.org; write to Gospel Light Worldwide, P.O. Box 3875, Ventura, CA 93006; or send an e-mail to info@gospellightworldwide.org.

DEDICATION

I gratefully dedicate this book to Falma Rufus, the international prayer coordinator for my ministry. Falma, you have helped me accomplish great exploits in the kingdom of God. Only the Lord and eternity will ever reveal the gratitude in my heart for your love and faithfulness. Thank you for being who you are and giving your time and life for God's purposes.

I also dedicate this book to the Wentroble Christian Ministries intercessors in Dallas, Texas. You are a team that is unsurpassed! God has heard the many hours of late-night prayers you have prayed. How thankful I am that the Lord put us together!

Thank you, Augusta Underwood, and the intercessors in Wichita, Kansas. Thank you, also, to the hundreds of other WCM intercessors who pray for me on a regular basis. This book is a result of your labor of love in intercession. You and the Lord made it happen. God gave me the best when He gave you to me!

May this book release intercessors around the world into a higher level of powerful prayer. May we continue together to help shape history through the awesome privilege of intercession.

Above all, I dedicate this book to the Lord Jesus Christ. Without You, I can do nothing. May You receive great glory and honor from a new breed of intercessors in the nations of the world.

CONTENTS

Individual Authority

As we allow Jesus (the Word) to live His life through us, we become the expression of Him in the earth. We, as living epistles, have the ability to slay the old Adamic nature and to live as an expression of the nature of Christ.

Corporate Authority

God began His purposes with an individual man, but He consummates them with a corporate people. Exponential power is released through corporate unity.

Territorial Authority

God promises that a strong, vibrant Church, operating in righteousness, has the ability through intercession to heal the land. As the Lord connects believers in a city or a region, exponential power is loosed to change the spiritual climate of the area.

The Right Time and the Right Season

Times of waiting often precede times of release. These times of waiting are not to be wasted but, rather, are to be filled with purpose. Intercession has a now time to cause the will of God to be released. At the strategic time, I AM releases the future into the present situation.

Decrees, Declarations and Proclamations

Words spoken in faith and boldness release things in the Father's heart that are not yet seen. Jesus taught His disciples to pray, "Thy Kingdom come, Thy will be done in earth, as it is in heaven"—faith-filled words, proclaiming God's will and purposes.

Angels

The Lord provides help for believers from powerful angelic beings. Angels do not do what we have been assigned to do; they are our assistants in warfare. Angels also provide protection for us as we engage the enemy.

The Harvest

The purpose of authority in intercession is to cause God's will to be done in the earth, which includes a mighty harvest of souls brought into salvation. The harvest of God is released through a powerful Church that brings transformation to cities and nations.

HELP! I NEED MORE POWER IN MY PRAYERS

The trip to Afghanistan had been planned for several months. I was traveling with a team of 20 medical specialists and we looked forward to going into the war-torn, poverty-stricken country to help alleviate some of the suffering. We also had a great expectation of bringing hope to the Afghans for a better tomorrow.

Afghanistan is a country in transition. Although the nation is no longer under the rule of the Taliban, it has not yet experienced all the changes necessary to make it whole. Poverty still abounds. Sickness and disease are everywhere. Buildings lie in ruin, and crime runs rampant.

How wonderful it was when we discovered a hotel available for us in Kabul! Due to the massive destruction from 25 years of war, we had anticipated the possibility of sleeping in a tent. A hotel—*any* hotel—would be better than that! We later laughed and told people we stayed in a five-star hotel; the only problem was that all the stars fell off.

At least we had running water and electricity—most of the time. However, we never knew when the power would go off. When the electricity was on, we could turn on fans to keep a small amount of air moving in the sweltering heat. We could use our hair dryers and turn on lights for reading or dressing. We truly counted our blessings because other parts of the city had been without electricity for many months.

INCONSISTENT POWER

I never was able to discover why the power in Afghanistan would be on for a while and then off for a period of time. If electricity was available, why didn't we have access to it all of the time? What caused the inconsistency?

Often I have had the same questions about my prayer life. Sometimes, when I am praying, the power of God seems almost tangible. Later, the answers to those prayers manifest in the situations I addressed. Other times, it seems like the heavens are brass. I pray every way I know to pray, but nothing seems to happen. The necessary power to produce the necessary results does not seem to be present. Situations remain the same, even though change and transformation desperately need to occur.

On one particular Sunday morning the power of prayer was evident in our home church. My husband, Dale, had been experiencing an annoying heart skip for many years. At times this would not occur for months. At other times it would skip beats several times a day. On this occasion his heart had been skipping beats throughout the day for a number of weeks. Dale was standing next to Chuck Pierce at our church, Glory of Zion, in Denton, Texas. Pastor Robert Heidler asked the people to turn and pray for the person next to them. Chuck laid a hand over Dale's heart and spoke to the condition: "I command this heart to beat normally."

Such a short prayer, yet such powerful results! The next day Dale's heart skipped only two beats; the day after, only one. Beginning on the third day, Dale's heart beat normally. It was obvious that transformation in his physical heart had occurred.

Why did this short, simple prayer suddenly get such powerful results?

Many prayers had been prayed over Dale's heart throughout the years. Why did this short, simple prayer suddenly get such powerful results when other prayers did not seem to change his situation?

I was speaking at a Bible school in Canada several years ago. For many years the students and faculty had been praying about the desire for a new facility. The student enrollment had increased, and the school needed more room to accommodate those wanting to attend.

One evening the school director, his wife and I drove to a nearby building that belonged to a church. We sat in the car in front of the facility for several minutes. The director explained the situation surrounding the possible sale of that building and property. Although the building was beautiful and fairly new, the attendance of the church was not large enough to continue to pay for it. Some of the members wanted to sell it to be free from the debt. Other members wanted to continue to hold the property in hopes of more income.

The three of us sat in the car and prayed:

Lord, You know the answer to this situation. We believe You
have the answer for the members of this church. We also believe
You have the answer for the Bible school. We believe You have
shown us that this building is to be used for the Bible school.
We therefore speak to this property and tell it to be released.
We now call it into the hands of this student body to train the
next generation. We speak release of debt to the members of this
church. We call forth the right facility that will meet their needs
and not entangle them with debt. Lord, we thank You now for
answering this prayer. Thank You that both the church and the
Bible school will be blessed in this transaction.

A few weeks later I received a phone call from the Bible
school director. "Barbara, I have to tell you what has happened,"
the director said. "Remember the church property we prayed
over? The members have come into agreement that they want to
sell the property to us. They have found a facility that will meet
their needs and free them from debt. There is unity and joy in
the congregation over this decision. Up until now, the whole
issue of the property was bringing division among the members.
Now they are excited at the Lord's provision."

When praying this kind of prayer, we have to truly seek
God's will for everyone involved, not just the solution that best
fits what we want at the moment. In this case, the answer was
best for both parties. If God had wanted the church to grow in
that facility, He would have provided another building for the
Bible school.

I was both thrilled and amazed. How often I had prayed over
similar situations and nothing happened. This time, there
seemed to be a power in the prayer that brought about resolu-
tion. Why wasn't there power like this each time I prayed?

Many times I have asked myself about the inconsistencies in
my prayer life:

- Why do my prayers sometimes fail to bring transformation to the subject of my prayers?
- Why are some people more effective than others in getting their prayers answered?
- Is there a way to increase the power in my prayers?
- Why should I want more power? Is it pride?
- Are there limitations to the effectiveness of my prayers?
- How can I tell the difference between a lack of prayer power and God simply saying "No" or "Not right now"?

God has many people who are faithful in prayer. These people love the Lord with all their hearts. However, they also realize that they need more power in their prayer lives because they just do not see the results for which they long in prayer.

HINDRANCES TO ANSWERED PRAYER

I must confess that I do not have all the answers to these questions about prayer. However, I have discovered some principles that give me a better understanding and make my prayers more effective.

Sin

One of the principles for releasing more power in prayer is to be sure our lives are as free from sin as possible. I am not speaking of sinless perfection. When I first read the Scripture that told me to be perfect (see Matt. 5:48), I thought it meant I was never to miss the mark. However, the word "perfect" in this Scripture really ly means "to complete thoroughly; to mend or to restore."[1] God wants us to be so complete in Him that we are fully restored to look and act like Him. He wants us to be mature children of God.

At the same time, God does not want us to practice habitual sin. He knows that sin brings destruction to our lives and separates us from fellowship with Him. Our prayers can be hindered by sin—particularly habitual sin—in our lives:

> If I regard iniquity in my heart, the Lord will not hear me (Ps. 66:18, *KJV*).

However, when we do sin, the Lord has made a way for us to be forgiven and restored. If we pray and "confess our sins, He is faithful and righteous to forgive us our sins and to cleanse us from all unrighteousness" (1 John 1:9).

God always hears our prayers; it is just the effectiveness of them and the answers that are hindered by sin. When we have confessed our sins and received the Lord's forgiveness, we can approach Him in prayer, knowing the barrier has been removed. We do not have to carry guilt and condemnation from past sins. We can then be God-conscious and not sin-conscious. What joy in knowing that we are forgiven, cleansed and free to fully participate with God in His plans!

Unbelief

Another hindrance to answered prayer is unbelief. After praying with someone, that person may respond, "I wish I could believe that God will do what you have prayed." God characterizes an unbelieving heart as an evil heart (see Heb. 3:12).

The Bible gives many examples of people who failed to receive God's blessings because of unbelief. In Romans we see that there were those who by their unbelief were cut off from God's promises. The writer tells us to not be ensnared by the same unbelief but to stand firm in our faith toward God (see 11:17-21).

Even when we have seen the goodness of the Lord toward our lives, we can find ourselves in seasons of unbelief. How do we end up in that state when God has been so good to us? One reason is that we tend to recall and obsess on our unworthiness.

We remember the mistakes we have made in the past. Our emotions and lives have told us that we are not worthy of God's blessings. Somehow we come into agreement with the unworthiness. What freedom when we come to understand fully that Jesus has made us righteous! We are not made worthy when we keep all the rules and regulations; we are made righteous because of our faith:

> Not having a righteousness of my own derived from the Law, but that which is through faith in Christ, the righteousness which comes from God on the basis of faith (Phil. 3:9).

A revelation of what Jesus has done for us will destroy the imprisonment of unworthiness.

Another area of unbelief arises when God seemingly answers the prayers of others but not our own. It is easy to believe God will answer the prayers of pastors, evangelists or leaders of ministry organizations. When they relate their stories of victories in prayer, they seem to be such powerful people. The problem is that frequently these people fail to honestly disclose the many prayers that have gone unanswered. I think that is one reason I love Scripture so much. Throughout the Bible, we read about people's failures as well as their victories.

Peter was a person who did not always do the right thing. He had an excellent revelation by the Spirit of God about who Jesus was. Then in the next breath he tried to talk Jesus out of doing God's will. Jesus had to say to Peter, "Get behind Me, Satan!" (Matt. 16:23). Peter was allowing the enemy to influence his thoughts. He was thinking in a carnal way rather than in God's way.

In spite of that, God still used Peter dynamically on the Day of Pentecost. He was able to preach a powerful sermon that resulted in 3,000 people being saved (see Acts 2:14-41). God empowers people to do powerful exploits for Him, though they are not usually the people we would choose. God will use whoever comes to Him with a heart that is set toward Him and His purposes. Let the Lord remove any place of doubt that is in you. Then pray and see what great things He will do through you!

Bad Religious Teachings

Our prayers can often be hindered due to unexamined or erroneous religious teachings. I grew up in a church that told me that many things in the Bible had ceased. I was taught that healings, supernatural signs and wonders, miracles and deliverance had ended with the early apostles. Therefore I never expected God to answer my prayers in an authoritative way. How surprised I was when He miraculously healed our youngest son of rectal polyps at the age of two! It no longer mattered that others told me God does not carry out miracles today. The Lord performed a miracle for our son—even the doctors confirmed it.

> *God is bigger than the box we attempt to put Him in.*

Lack of Knowledge

Another hindrance to getting answers to prayers is a lack of knowledge. The Lord desires to free us from small thinking. He is bigger than the box we attempt to put Him in. He is the same yesterday, today and forever (see Heb. 13:8). We can pray and see the authority of God perform miraculous deeds today.

Sometimes we have tunnel vision. Due to our lack of knowledge, we are aware only of what is happening around us. If we are not established in present truth, we may not be aware of some of the things God is doing around the world (see 2 Pet. 1:12). We are living in days of restoration. God is restoring much that occurred during New Testament days. Just because we do not see it where we live does not mean it is not happening.

We tend to think that revival is not occurring because it is not happening in our church or city. However, Christianity today is growing rapidly in many places and remains the largest religious faith in the world. The church in China is adding 25,000 new members each day. Nigeria is experiencing phenomenal church growth. Monthly prayer meetings in one area of that nation include almost half a million people. Redeemed Church of God is the size of 86 football fields. It is the equivalent to Denver's Mile High Stadium being filled nearly four times.

The Bible tells us that God's people perish, or are destroyed, due to a lack of knowledge (see Hos. 4:6). Keeping alert to what is happening throughout the world in the Body of Christ will help dismantle our unbelief.

Disunity

Another thing that hinders answered prayer is disunity. Throughout history great leaders have understood the power of unity. Unity can be used for good or evil. The results are different depending on the intent of the unity. At the tower of Babel, unity was used for evil purposes:

> The LORD said, "Behold, they are one people, and they all have the same language. And this is what they began to do, and now nothing which they purpose to do will be impossible for them" (Gen. 11:6).

The power of unity caused them to be able to do anything they proposed, even though it was with evil intent.

Osama bin Laden knows the power of unity. His networking of the al-Qaeda terrorist cells released a power that was able to destroy the Twin Towers in New York City on September 11, 2001.

Unity, even for evil purposes, is indeed a powerful force.

When God's people walk in unity, however, the corporate prayers of the united group releases power to bring positive change and transformation (see Ps. 133). Dutch Sheets, along with other writers, tracked how much prayer accompanied the United States presidential election of 2000. One of the strengths in the election was the unity of intercessors and church leaders throughout the Body of Christ. Dutch wrote:

> I also saw as never before the value of cooperation and unity in the body of Christ. If God had not been establishing the communications infrastructure through the global prayer movement during the past decade, I don't think we would have been able to accomplish what we did. The following examples show the crucial roles these had during this season of intercession.

- I sought confirmation from other spiritual leaders on the accuracy of the burden, as well as how to communicate it.
- Many leaders, key ministries, and thousands of people helped to distribute the alert.
- Pastors incorporated much more prayer than usual for the elections into their services and into the overall lives of their churches.
- In Florida, where the battle was so intense, churches, leaders, and intercessors joined together in an unprecedented way. Their unity and perseverance were superb.[2]

Lack of Understanding

One more hindrance to answered prayer is a lack of understanding of authority, which is the primary subject of this book. Over and over again we see ourselves as insignificant and powerless; therefore, we fail to use the authority that Jesus purchased for us at Calvary. After His death, burial and resurrection, Jesus gave authority to those who would follow Him:

> I will give you the keys of the kingdom of heaven; and whatever you shall bind on earth have been bound in heaven, and whatever you loose on earth have been loosed in heaven (Matt. 16:19).

The keys Jesus gave to His followers have the authority to forbid and to allow. In prayer, we can forbid, or bind, those things that are contrary to the will of God. We can also allow, or loose, the will of God to manifest itself on Earth. God's will is not the abuse of women, the use of children for evil purposes, poverty, sickness or other evils. His will on Earth is to look like His will in heaven (see Matt. 6:10).

The Lord is even interested in things that do not seem spiritual to us. If these things are part of our lives, He is interested in them because He is interested in us. My husband, Dale, works as an engineer for a manufacturing plant. One time the workers were having difficulty with one of the machines. Although all the experts and maintenance people had tried to solve the problem, the equipment still failed to function properly. One day Dale told another worker that he was going to pray about the machine.

> *After His death, burial and resurrection, Jesus gave authority to those who would follow Him.*

"I'm sure the Lord is not interested in mechanical equipment," the coworker quipped.

"Oh, yes, He is," Dale responded. "He is interested in every-thing that concerns me."

A few days later in a staff meeting, Dale gave a good report about the equipment. After praying, the equipment had been "healed." Dale shared with the group that God was interested in the equipment because it was a concern to Dale. The Lord gives us authority over all of creation. A mandate to rule with authority is given in the Garden (see Gen. 1:26-28). Jesus sharpens that man-date in the New Testament (see Matt. 28:18-20). Understanding this authority helps us pray effectively in order to release needed changes.

Christians wielding authority in ungodly ways can deeply wound people. Authority is not intended by God to harm us but to protect us and bring God's will to Earth. God's authority is not abusive. If we are truly operating in God's authority, we will not abuse our spouses, our children or anyone else. We will not use our authority to abuse people who work for us. We will not even abuse the land on which we live. We will use God's del-egated authority for good, not for evil.

A HIGHER LEVEL

A proper understanding of God's authority will release us into higher levels of intercession. Authority is involved in causing the will of God to manifest itself on Earth. You may want to pray this prayer to prepare your heart for an advancement in intercession:

Father in heaven, I thank You that I can come to You in prayer. Help! I need more power in my prayers. Please forgive me and cleanse me of all unrighteousness in my life. Search my heart by the power of the Holy Spirit. Remove anything that hinders me in my prayer life. Forgive me and deliver me from all unbe-lief. I confess that You are the same yesterday, today and forev-

er. Nothing is too difficult for You. Reveal to me Your mighty power from Your Word. Give me an understanding of present-day truth and Your mighty deeds. Let me be an instrument of unity in Your body. Lead me to others with whom I need to connect. I want to join with them in praying corporately for Your purposes to be released on Earth. Thank You that You are interested in everything that concerns me. I am asking You to release a higher level of authority in my prayers. May I pray prayers that get results. I submit to Your authority and to the authorities You have placed in my life. Be glorified as Your will is released on Earth, even as it is in heaven. I pray all of this in Jesus' name. Amen!

Notes
1. James Strong, *The Exhaustive Concordance of the Bible: Greek Dictionary of the New Testament* (McLean, VA: MacDonald Publishing Company, n.d.), p. 40.
2. Dutch Sheets, "Opening the Door to the White House," in *Destiny of a Nation*, ed. C. Peter Wagner (Colorado Springs, CO: Wagner Publications, 2001), pp. 79-80.

CHAPTER 2

UNDERSTANDING
AUTHORITY

For several years I took ministry teams into Russia. We conducted pastors' conferences that included the pastors, their
spouses and their children. These pastors and their families
came from a number of villages around St. Petersburg. Pastors
and church leaders in Russia work very hard and seldom take
time to rest. Their families often suffer as a result. The conferences were called Pastors' Holidays and were designed not only
for teaching and ministry but also for recreation and fellowship.

In a number of Russian villages our group also sponsored
International Christian Festivals. The purpose of the festivals
was evangelism and church planting. Excitement reverberated
throughout the crowds when entire villages received Jesus as
Savior, and we established churches for the new believers.

Each time we went to Russia we attended the ballet and visited museums and other cultural sites. One thing that made a distinct impression on me as we visited this beautiful yet neglected land was the emotional scars and deprivation in the lives of the citizens, caused by authorities in the past. Russians are by nature exceptionally warm, creative people. Yet they have never been able to come into their full potential. One reason for this is that so many of their rulers—even those who professed Orthodox Christianity—have, for the most part, abused power and violated God's system of authority.

Ungodly Leadership

There can be no governing authority except that which God establishes (see Rom. 13:1). God created the idea of government, rulers and authority! However, this—as history so clearly and utterly verifies—does not mean that all leaders will follow God's plan, properly using the authority and power they have been given. Russia's roll call of leaders—the czars, Stalin, Lenin, et al.—provide the proof. Ivan the Terrible, who was crowned czar in 1547, was a repressive dictator. His line of czarist leadership and abuse of the people continued until the 1917 Russian Revolution. At that time the Bolsheviks came into power as the first Soviet government. They established a new, experimental communist system based on the writings of Karl Marx. A bitter civil war followed, and the government seized all private property. Stalin followed Lenin as leader and initiated a series of political purges that lasted through the 1930s. The Soviet Union became involved in World War II and lost more than 20 million people. Cities and the countryside were devastated during this period.[1]

Since the breakup of the Soviet Union in 1991, several leaders have made attempts to bring hope and prosperity to Russia despite its history of death, destruction and discouragement. Russia, moreover, is not the only country experiencing the effects of a government that does not operate under God's pattern of authority. Throughout the world and throughout history, we see nations that suffer the consequences of ungodly leadership.

Operating under God's pattern of authority and guidance is different from a theocracy where a ruler claims absolute divine authority. The Old Testament offers examples of a kind of theocracy, and Jesus will someday rule with absolute divine authority. But in calling for godly leadership, I am not suggesting that we need earthly theocracies today. Since New Testament days, we have seen horrific examples of ungodly theocracies—the Taliban, Ayatollahs and to some degree certain mistaken medieval church leaders, just to name a few.

God gives people a spiritual choice and He will not usurp the will of the people. However, when laws and principles are broken, consequences will follow.

"AUTHORITY" DEFINED

What is authority? *Webster's New World College Dictionary* defines it as "the power or right to give commands, enforce obedience, take action, or make final decisions; jurisdiction."[2] It also means "such power as delegated to another; authorization."[3] Of course, God is the ultimate authority and, as shown in Romans 13:1, He is the authority giver.

Authority itself is not wrong. From the beginning of time God commanded man to exercise authority on Earth:

And God said, Let us make man in our image, after our likeness: and let them have dominion over the fish of the sea, and over the fowl of the air, and over the cattle, and over all the earth, and over every creeping thing that creepeth upon the earth. So God created man in his own image, in the image of God created he him; male and female created he them. And God blessed them, and God said unto them, Be fruitful, and multiply, and replenish the earth, and subdue it: and have dominion over the fish of the sea, and over the fowl of the air, and over every living thing that moveth upon the earth (Gen. 1:26-28, *KJV*).

> *From the beginning, God commanded man to exercise authority on Earth.*

Although God issued a mandate for man to rule on Earth, the intention has always been that man should be under God's authority. Authority has always been a subject of controversy in the universe. Satan tried to usurp God's authority and led both angels and mankind in rebellion (see Gen. 3:1-5; Isa. 14:12-15; Ezek. 28:13-17). Even today, millions of evil spirits (fallen angels that rebelled with Satan) and people (sinners who succumb to Satan's lies) operate on Earth in opposition to God's authority. When a ruler abuses power and position conferred by God, he or she also lapses into rebellion—and sometimes into outright defiance.

AUTHORITY OVER REBELLION

As believers, once we have come under God's authority, we are able to pray with His authority. God speaks to people who are in relationship with Him. He gives them revelation of His will. The revelation of His will releases in believers the authority to speak forth His will in a situation. Therefore, revelation releases authority.

God gave revelation to Moses during a face-to-face encounter. Through the revelation God gave him, Moses received authority.

Aaron and Miriam, the brother and sister of Moses, rebelled against that authority. God then spoke to them and reprimanded them for rebelling against His delegated authority (see Num. 12). Watchman Nee, in his book *Spiritual Authority*, admonished us to seek God and not to strive for authority:

> When we seek the face of our Lord, He gives us revelation and establishes our authority.
>
> Revelation is therefore the evidence of authority. We must learn not to strive or speak for ourselves. We should not join the ranks of Aaron and Miriam in struggling for authority. Indeed, if we strive, it only proves that our authority is wholly carnal, dark and void of heavenly vision.[4]

AUTHORITY IN GOD'S TIME

Throughout the Bible, godly leaders who received revelation from the Lord act as examples of the effects of authoritative power. Joseph was one who looked to God for wisdom. As a young man, Joseph received a dream from the Lord, indicating his future role as a leader. It was not until many years later that the dream came to pass. Joseph lived through horrible adversity and seemingly impossible situations before stepping into his destiny. Throughout those difficult years, he continued to trust in the Lord. His future depended upon his being faithful to God in every circumstance of life. Purity of heart and life are essential if anyone given power or position on Earth is to succeed in exercising his or her responsibilities in a way that would honor God and truly benefit those under his or her authority.

Joseph rose to a remarkable height of political power in Egypt. During this era Egypt was one of the mightiest nations in the world. Spiros Zodhiates, in *Hebrew-Greek Key Study Bible*, describes Joseph's position during that time:

> Besides the personal ring and fine clothing, which
> Pharaoh gave him, he also placed him in the second
> chariot for a public procession. Kings often went out to
> battle with two chariots. One for the battle and the other
> to return home in case of disaster. The fact that Joseph
> rode in the second chariot would seem to indicate that
> he was second in command. In Gen. 42:6 he is also called
> the governor over the land. Therefore, he was in charge
> of the practical matters of administration in everyday
> life in Egypt.[5]

God gave Joseph wisdom. As a leader he was able to enact a
program that provided food for pagan and idolatrous Egypt as
well as his own family during a time of severe famine. Joseph's
authority was used to benefit the people and to release God's
blessings upon them. Good leadership always seeks the best for
the people and the nation. Job 34:17 asks, "Shall one who hates
justice rule?" emphasizing the need for leaders who have pure
motives and will institute just laws.

Restoration and Fulfillment
Nehemiah was another person God used to bless His people.
Nehemiah lived in luxury as the cupbearer to King Artaxerxes.
After hearing about the deplorable conditions in Jerusalem and
the attacks from the enemy on God's people, Nehemiah was
appointed by the Persians to be governor of Jerusalem. He came
to accomplish God's purpose with an army escort financed by
the Persian government. He was an amazing spiritual leader who
operated in very practical ways. Despite the attacks from surrounding enemies, Nehemiah was able to operate in an authority that brought full restoration to the city.

Nehemiah was a leader who maintained a life of deep prayer and intercession (see Neh. 1). His constant seeking of the Lord resulted in an ability to accomplish in a very short time that which had not been accomplished in more than 100 years. Prayer releases insight to govern the affairs of life, and causes the will of God to be fulfilled.

Wisdom

At first, King Solomon sought the Lord for wisdom in exercising authority over the people. God appeared to Solomon in a dream and said, "Ask what you wish me to give you"(1 Kings 3:5). Solomon responded to the Lord:

> "Now, O LORD my God, You have made Your servant king in place of my father David, yet I am but a little child; I do not know how to go out or come in. Your servant is in the midst of Your people which You have chosen, a great people who are too many to be numbered or counted. So give Your servant an understanding heart to judge Your people to discern between good and evil. For who is able to judge this great people of Yours?"
>
> It was pleasing in the sight of the Lord that Solomon had asked this thing. God said to him, "Because you have asked this thing and have not asked for yourself long life, nor have asked riches for yourself, nor have you asked for the life of your enemies, but have asked for yourself discernment to understand justice, behold, I have done according to your words. Behold, I have given you a wise and discerning heart, so that there has been no one like you before you, nor shall one like you arise after you. I have also given you what you have not asked, both riches and honor, so that there will not be any among the kings like you all your days" (vv. 7-13).

Solomon's discerning heart—put there by God—gave him the ability to make decisions that amazed the people. He was also able to implement a plan that resulted in such great wealth that it was heard about in faraway nations. King Solomon humbly asked God for an ability to judge between good and evil in the people. He did not ask for selfish rewards. However, a pure heart that seeks the Lord for wisdom in judging between good and evil will result in a life that also receives great

> *The right kind of authority requires a heart that has been purified.*

blessings from the Lord. (How sad that Solomon later allowed his heart to be drawn into idolatry through his marriages to 300 wives and 700 concubines.)

The right kind of authority requires a heart that has been purified. A right and pure heart is dependent on the Lord for wisdom and continually seeks to know how to judge between good and evil. The desire for God's purposes to be accomplished will at all times be foremost. Our motives and attitudes must forever be for God's will to be done.

God is the One who has authoritative power over all of creation. His rule should direct every part of life and creation. Due to sin and rebellion, we do not see the full manifestation of God's rule today. However, Isaiah 9:7 assures us that the supreme rule of the Lord will one day be established on Earth: "There will be no end to the increase of His government or of peace."[6]

Government

God put His authority to govern in His creation. We see examples of this in the animal kingdom. Lions rule over smaller animals. Roosters rule over chickens. Cats rule over mice. The list is endless, but it is evident that God put an innate authority within animals to rule, or govern.

God put the authority to govern in created objects. Sun, moon, stars, mountains, valleys and seas rule over their given assignments.

- **Sun, moon and stars:** "God made the two great lights, the greater light to govern the day, and the lesser light to govern the night; He made the stars also. God placed them in the expanse of the heavens to give light on the earth, and to govern the day and the night, and to separate the light from the darkness; and God saw that it was good" (Gen. 1:16-18).
- **Mountains and valleys:** "The mountains rose; the valleys sank down to the place which You established for them. You set a boundary that they may not pass over, so that they will not return to cover the earth" (Ps. 104:8-9).
- **Seas:** "He set for the sea its boundary so that the water would not transgress His command" (Prov. 8:29).

God has also placed the authority to rule in government:

Every person is to be in subjection to the governing authorities. For there is no authority except from God, and those which exist are established by God (Rom. 13:1).

The purpose of civil government is to carry out the desires of God so that righteousness, rather than evil, can reign on Earth:

Surely I will require your lifeblood; from every beast I will require it. And from every man, from every man's brother I will require the life of man. Whoever sheds man's blood, by man his blood shall be shed, for in the image of God He made man (Gen. 9:5-6).

According to Scripture, our rulers are accountable to God for how they use the authority He has given to them. Ruling in the fear of the Lord brings extraordinary delight to those who are under their jurisdiction:

By me princes rule, and nobles, all who judge rightly (Prov. 8:16).

The God of Israel said, the Rock of Israel spoke to me, "He who rules over men righteously, who rules in the fear of God, is as the light of the morning when the sun rises, a morning without clouds, when the tender grass springs out of the earth, through sunshine after rain" (2 Sam. 23:3-4).

SPIRITUAL GOVERNMENT

Not only did God establish earthly governments, but He also ordained spiritual government. Throughout the Old Testament we find priests and prophets ministering in places of worship. They were also responsible for governing the conduct of the people under their charge.

In the New Testament, after the death, burial and resurrection of Jesus, a new order of spiritual government was established:

And He gave some as apostles, and some as prophets, and some as evangelists, and some as pastors and teachers (Eph. 4:11).

The purpose of this New Testament government is to teach, train, shepherd and help bring the people of God into spiritual maturity. Christians are admonished to listen to and obey these God-established leaders:

Obey your leaders and submit to them, for they keep watch over your souls as those who will give an account. Let them do this with joy and not with grief, for this would be unprofitable for you (Heb. 13:17).

Spiritual government is actually the government of God that has been delegated to certain individuals in the Church:

For a child will be born to us, a son will be given to us; and the government will rest on His shoulders; and His name will be called Wonderful Counselor, Mighty God, Eternal Father, Prince of Peace (Isa. 9:6).

The Bible refers to Christians as the Body of Christ. Christ's shoulders are the governmental leaders in the Church. God's government is placed in the hands of these spiritual leaders. They have power of authority under the Lord's direction and are to rule with Christlike humility.

Self-Governing Authority

Another realm of authority is self-governing, which we each do as individuals. Along with all other areas of delegated authority, this should be subject to God's authority. Otherwise, authority can be used to hurt, abuse or destroy.

God's authority delegated in the Garden was for the purpose of extending His kingdom. The kingdom of God was not destined to remain merely in the Garden; it was to be extended until it filled the whole Earth. Man was given the authority to fulfill God's heavenly mandate. However, due to man's rebellion against God, man lost his authority.

Jesus came to restore everything that was lost in the fall of mankind. As humanity's true representative, Jesus is restoring our original purpose and authority (see Heb. 2:5-18). He has restored the mandate to extend the kingdom of God into all the world (see Matt. 28:18-20). As we exercise the authority delegated to us by Jesus in intercession, we participate in extending the will of God on Earth. We speak His will and have the authority to be His voice throughout the world. His will is that His authority be acknowledged in all nations and by all people!

Pray, then, in this way: "Our Father who is in heaven, hallowed be Your name. Your kingdom come. Your will be done, on earth as it is in heaven" (Matt. 6:9-10).

You may want to pray the following prayer:

Heavenly Father, thank You that You have all authority and all power, both in heaven and on Earth. I desire to be like You. Therefore, I am asking You to grace me to forgive all authority figures who have used authority in wrong ways in my life. I choose to forgive them in Jesus' name. Open my spiritual eyes to see and understand that Your authority is to be used for good purposes, not for evil purposes. Give me a greater level of authority in intercession. Help me to be Your voice on Earth. I will speak Your Word in intercession and expect to see it made manifest. Thank You for allowing me to participate in implementing Your will on Earth. In Jesus' name I pray. Amen.

Notes

1. Jon M. Leverenz and Brett R. Gover, eds., *The World: Afghanistan to Zimbabwe* (Skokie, IL: Rand McNally, 1996), p. 155.
2. *Webster's New World College Dictionary*, 4th ed., s.v. "authority."
3. Ibid.
4. Watchman Nee, *Spiritual Authority* (New York: Christian Fellowship Publishers, Inc., 1972), p. 129.

5. Spiros Zodhiates, *Hebrew-Greek Keyword Study Bible (New American Standard Version)* (Chattanooga, TN: AMG Publishers, 1990), p. 62.

6. This passage establishes a messianic reign which the New Testament recognizes as having begun with Jesus Christ—the fullest manifestation of which must wait until the Second Coming.

IDENTIFYING BOUNDARIES

My nephew Scott—at the time a very busy two-year-old—came with his parents to visit for a few days. My son, Brian, was three and was also a very busy little boy. At the beginning of the visit, both cousins were happy to see each other. Having someone to play with was exciting for a little while—until they each wanted to play with the same toy at the same time.

Scott soon discovered a little car of Brian's that he really liked. When Brian noticed Scott playing with it, he immediately cried out, "Mine!" Scott was not about to give up easily, so he yelled back, "Mine!" Both boys felt they had a right to the car—Brian because he was the legal owner and Scott because he was the one who had possession of it. The battle was on!

For several days the boys ran into the same dilemma. Finally Brian learned the rules. If Scott picked up the car first, he had a right to play with it; Brian would have to wait until Scott found something else with which to play. Otherwise Brian would be in trouble with his mother. However, Brian was not to be deterred from his mission of obtaining what he felt was legally his. He discovered that if he would hand Scott his favorite blanket, he could then retrieve the car at the same time. Distracted, Scott would not cry. By doing this, Brian could get his car while the blanket sidetracked Scott.

Brian was learning about boundaries at an early age. There were boundaries that he could not cross without suffering the consequences. He also learned that in order to enlarge present boundaries he would have to develop strategy and wisdom. He did not have a right to infringe on another person's boundaries.

Assigned Boundaries

Intercessors must also learn to identify the boundaries the Lord has assigned to them. Some intercessors are assigned to individuals. Others are assigned to their local church or pastor. Often intercessors are assigned to cities, states, nations or people groups. Authority from the Lord is given within each assigned boundary, so the intercessor can be successful in fulfilling the task.

What exactly are boundaries? The dictionary defines the word "boundary" as "any line or thing marking a limit; bound; border."[1] States and nations have borders. Cities, counties and time zones all have geographical borders or boundaries.

The laws within one state may be different from the laws in another state. The borders of the state define where certain laws operate. I do not always know what the law is regarding seat belts in various states where I travel. Texas requires seat belts to be buckled around people in only the front seat of a vehicle. Other states require seat belts to be fastened around people throughout the car. Since I do not always know the law for the state I am in, I try to remember to buckle my seat belt whenever I am in a car. By doing this I am operating legally, regardless of the law within the state boundary.

Throughout the Bible we see where the Lord established boundaries for geographical locations:

> When the Most High gave the nations their inheritance, when He separated the sons of man, He set the boundaries of the peoples according to the number of the sons of Israel (Deut. 32:8).

> You set a boundary that they may not pass over, so that they will not return to cover the earth (Ps. 104:9).

> "Do you not fear Me?" declares the LORD. "Do you not tremble in My presence? For I have placed the sand as a boundary for the sea, an eternal decree, so it cannot cross over it. Though the waves toss, yet they cannot prevail; though they roar, yet they cannot cross over it" (Jer. 5:22).

> And He made from one man every nation of mankind to live on all the face of the earth, having determined their appointed times and the boundaries of their habitation (Acts 17:26).

Boundaries define a particular jurisdiction or domain. When I was in nursing school, I had a roommate who never seemed to understand boundaries. Whenever I would go home for a weekend, I usually could predict what I would find when

I returned to my dorm room: Her things would be piled on my side of the room! Since she was never there when I returned, I would spend the first 30 minutes cleaning her clothes off my bed, her papers off my desk and emptying the trash she left scattered on my side of the room. Her boundaries constantly expanded throughout the room when I was gone. The bathroom was another story in itself!

The Need

The Bible is full of stories about boundaries. In the Old Testament we read about cities that had walls around their borders. These walls served two purposes. The first was to protect the inhabitants inside the city. Anyone coming into the city was required to enter through the gates. The gatekeepers had the authority to determine who could come and go from the city. Access to the city was therefore limited. The second reason for the walls was to limit the enemy and keep him outside. Whether the enemy consisted of people or wild animals, none could come and go at will. All needed permission to enter the boundaries of the territory.

Nehemiah was a man in the Old Testament who understood the importance of guarding the boundaries of a city. Artaxerxes, the pagan king, had set God's people free from Babylonian captivity, and a remnant of them had returned to the city of Jerusalem and rebuilt the Temple of the Lord. However, they never rebuilt the walls around the borders of the city. Since the walls were down and the gates had been burned with fire, the enemy had access to the city. Nehemiah left the comfort of the king's palace in Susa and went to Jerusalem because he had a burden from the Lord to see the walls restored.

The first thing Nehemiah did before exercising his authority over the borders of Jerusalem was to pray. He asked the Lord to cleanse and forgive him and his forefathers who had sinned against God. He confessed that his people had failed to guard the boundaries of the city and the boundaries of their covenant with the Lord. They were therefore scattered, due to their disobedience. Nehemiah also reminded the Lord of His promise of restoration for those who would turn to Him.

When a former generation fails to guard cities and nations, the Lord always looks for a remnant of people who will choose to return to Him. As confession and repentance are made to the Lord for former sins in that territory, an opening becomes available for restoration and healing of

> *Failure to operate within God's limits of authority in intercession can bring tragedy.*

the land. Authority is restored for interceding and guarding the boundaries of the territory.

Protection and Respect

Failure to operate within God's limits of authority in intercession can bring tragedy. God does not give intercessors authority over another person's will. The Lord will not take away a person's ability to choose. He gives people a will and the freedom to exercise it. Otherwise they would be robots. Failure to respect these boundaries can greatly hinder or even torpedo intercession. Throughout the Bible God's people are told to choose:

> Choose for yourselves today whom you will serve: whether the gods which your fathers served which were beyond the River, or the gods of the Amorites in whose land you are living; but as for me and my house, we will serve the LORD (Josh. 24:15).

> Choose a man for yourselves and let him come down to me (1 Sam. 17:8).

> By faith Moses, when he had grown up, refused to be
> called the son of Pharaoh's daughter, choosing rather
> to endure ill-treatment with the people of God than to
> enjoy the passing pleasures of sin (Heb. 11:24-25).

Whenever intercessors use prayer to transcend another person's will, the intercessors have failed to identify the borders of their authority. They have actually stepped into a form of witchcraft. Witchcraft seeks to control and manipulate people so that they are no longer able to will to do what they choose. This is why some people must be set free from the power of the enemy before they can choose to obey the Lord. They may want the Lord's will but still be unable to choose to follow it. Freeing people restores their ability to choose. In her book *How to Cast Out Demons*, Doris Wagner addresses the issue of the inability to choose:

> Is the person in control, or does the phrase continually
> repeat, "I have prayed and confessed and cried but I can
> not get the victory over this besetting sin." When praying, confessing, and crying are not quite enough, it is a
> pretty good clue that perhaps a demonic presence is
> involved. In other words, the person does not control
> that particular problem, but the problem controls the
> person.[2]

The delegated authority of the Lord in intercession does not include the authority to change another person's will. However, we do have the authority to bind the demonic forces that influence other people:

> Truly I say to you, whatever you bind on earth shall have
> been bound in heaven; and whatever you loose on earth
> shall have been loosed in heaven (Matt. 18:18).

Once the spirits operating within a person are bound, that person is free to choose to obey or disobey the Lord.

Dean Sherman, in his book *Spiritual Warfare for Every Christian*, discusses the role of the intercessor who guards the boundaries of people or places in order to limit the activity of the enemy, as well as hold back God's judgment:

> We stand between the object of our intercession and God; or between the object and the devil.
>
> When we intercede between the object and God, we make specific requests for provision, protection, direction, or blessings from God on behalf of the person, place, or thing for which we are praying. We also stand between the object and God in order to hinder and slow His judgment. In many cases, the only reason God has not sent judgment is because we are interceding on behalf of the world and those in it. Not that we are more merciful than God is. He always longs to show mercy wherever possible. Our prayers give Him just cause to delay judgment and extend more opportunity for individuals to repent (see Exod. 32:32; 2 Pet. 2:9; Gen. 18:16-33).[3]

We also see the principle of guarding boundaries in the story of the Garden:

> Then the LORD God took the man and put him into the garden of Eden to cultivate it and keep it (Gen. 2:15).

The word "keep" in Hebrew is *shamar*. Some of the meanings of shamar are "to hedge around something (as with thorns), to guard, to watch (as a watchman of sheep or cattle), as a prophet, to keep safe, to protect. The word gives the idea of a sense of tending or exercising great care."[4]

Intercessors are to exercise great care over the boundaries of intercession the Lord has assigned to them. The authority to guard these boundaries comes with the assignment. The Lord will not ask us to do something and then fail to equip us for the task.

THE CHURCH'S WAKE-UP CALL

Too often Christians fail to guard the boundaries of their cities or territories. Some of us believe that the world is evil, and we should not be involved in it. A few even use Scripture to justify the reason they have distanced themselves from all activities outside the church walls. Here is an example:

> "Therefore, come out from their midst and be separate," says the Lord. "And do not touch what is unclean; and I will welcome you" (2 Cor. 6:17).

Taking this verse and others out of context and the lack of revelation concerning our mandate from the Lord to extend God's rule throughout the world (see Gen. 1:26-28) have caused many Christians to fail in guarding boundaries of an area. As a result of this neglect, individuals and society in general suffer the consequences, which include poverty, sickness, crime, perversion, drug addiction and numerous other evil situations. The enemy has had centuries of access to cities and individuals, but today the Church is receiving a wake-up call to arise and use our God-given authority in intercession.

The Lord will not ask us to do something and then fail to equip us for the task.

The psalmist David understood this principle:

The LORD says to my Lord: "Sit at My right hand until I make Your enemies a footstool for Your feet." The LORD will stretch forth Your strong scepter from Zion, saying, "Rule in the midst of Your enemies" (Ps. 110:1-2).

We are not involved in human conflict. We are involved in a spiritual battle and must use spiritual weapons (see Eph. 6:10-17). These weapons are powerful and more than adequate to accomplish the task. Using these weapons helps us to be able to destroy everything the enemy raises up in opposition to the lordship of Jesus Christ.

The enemy does not want us to accomplish this assignment from the Lord. He will use every device he can to hinder the intercessor or bring discouragement. If the enemy can keep us focused on our own set of problems, we will fail to guard the boundaries God has given us. Satan will even allow us to pray for our own needs, as long as we are not guarding the boundaries of other individuals or territories.

Intercessors are priests who are given the wonderful assignment of guarding boundaries. Guarding includes ruling. In her book *The Law of Boundaries*, Patti Amsden writes about boundaries:

Rulership is not a thing to be avoided. Rulership is intrinsically tied to boundaries. If you own it, you rule it. If you allow someone else to rule what you own, you are not being humble and lowly, you are being either slothful or foolish; and you will answer to God for your stewardship of that which He entrusted to your keeping. God told Adam to rule. In Adam's case, poor stewarding produced negative sanctions, extra burdens upon his labors, and loss of boundaries. But, even post-fall, Adam still had an earth to rule and boundaries to guard. Even a man in prison, having lost all possessions and freedom, must still rule and guard his own body and soul.[5]

REWARDS FOR THE FAITHFUL

There are rewards for those who are faithful to guard their boundaries in intercession. The assigned boundaries can be enlarged when the Lord orders an enlargement. Often when we are faithful in the small task He has given us, He will then enlarge our borders and give us a greater assignment:

> His master said to him, "Well done, good and faithful slave. You were faithful with a few things, I will put you in charge of many things; enter into the joy of your master" (Matt. 25:21).

Falma Rufus is the international prayer coordinator for Wentroble Christian Ministries and International Breakthrough Ministries. She began interceding by praying for her family and friends. As she was faithful in intercession, the Lord linked her with other intercessors to pray for churches and for our city. She continued to be faithful in her assignment to guard the borders against the enemy.

Often when we are faithful in a small task, God will then enlarge our borders.

Later she began coming to our intercession group to pray for the ministry each month. Her determination to watch over me and this ministry through intercession was evident to all. When the time came to appoint a new intercessory leader for our ministry, Falma was the obvious choice. She now leads our local intercessors several times each month and also oversees our ministry of intercessors worldwide. Being faithful to identify and guard the boundaries God assigned her has made Falma a role model for many in the Body of Christ.

YOUR ASSIGNED BOUNDARIES

Ask the Lord to identify the boundaries He has called you to guard. Some of these boundaries may include

- your family;
- your friends;
- pastors, missionaries or ministry leaders;
- your city, county or state;
- your nation, another nation or several nations;
- a people group such as Jews, Hispanics or African-Americans;
- a business or marketplace person;
- local or national civil governments;
- banking and economic institutions;
- arts and entertainment companies or industries;
- educational systems; or
- medical and professional groups.

You may be assigned to other people or groups that are not noted here. Whatever your assignment is, God will use you as a world changer to guard boundaries against the invasion of the enemy's plans. Once you are able to identify the boundaries God has given you to guard, you may want to pray the following prayer:

Father, I thank You for calling me to be an instrument of prayer. I want to see Your kingdom extended to the whole Earth. Show me the areas You have assigned for me to guard. By the power of Your Holy Spirit I receive the spiritual weapons needed to fulfill my assignment. If I should forget, please remind me to guard my God-given boundaries. I want to be faithful, both to You and to those for whom I am praying. I thank You for helping me not only to discern the tactics of the enemy but also to have the wisdom of God. May my words in intercession and warfare release Your authority to dismantle the plans of the enemy. May Your kingdom come on Earth, even as it is in heaven. In Jesus' name I pray. Amen.

Notes
1. *Webster's New World College Dictionary,* 4th ed., s.v. "boundary."
2. Doris M. Wagner, *How to Cast Out Demons: A Beginner's Guide* (Colorado Springs, CO: Wagner Institute for Practical Ministry, 1999), p. 47.
3. Dean Sherman, *Spiritual Warfare for Every Christian* (Seattle, WA: Frontline Communications, 1990), p. 157.
4. Spiros Zodhiates, *Hebrew-Greek Keyword Study Bible (New American Standard Version)* (Chattanooga, TN: AMG Publishers, 1990), p. 1787.
5. Patti Amsden, *The Law of Boundaries* (Kirkwood, MO: Impact Christian Books, Inc., 1999), p. 40.

CHAPTER 4

THE SPIRIT OF BOLDNESS

Throughout history heroes have typically been people who exhibited great boldness and courage in times of difficulty. One of my favorite people who exemplified those characteristics is Corrie ten Boom. Reading stories about her time spent in the concentration camps during World War II is a source of strength to me.

One story that revealed the grace of God upon Corrie and her sister, Betsie, recounts the time when they were in Ravensbrück. The guards constantly intimidated the female prisoners. They would parade them naked to the showers. At other times the guards would have them stand for hours at attention in rain-soaked fields. Being placed close to the barracks in which they could hear the screams of prisoners being tortured caused immense fear. Cruel treatment throughout their imprisonment was the norm.

Corrie and Betsie were strong believers. The Lord supernaturally allowed them to hide a Bible, medicine and a sweater. The barracks in which they were housed was infested with fleas. During their stay, they learned the power of giving thanks to the Lord in every situation. Not understanding why they should be thankful for the fleas, they thanked the Lord anyway.

Corrie and Betsie conducted Bible studies during the evenings in their dormitory room. Profound boldness filled their hearts in the midst of the terrifying living conditions:

> At first Betsie and I called these meetings with great timidity. However, as night after night went by and no guard ever came near us, we grew bolder. So many now wanted to join us that we held a second service after evening roll call. There on the *Lagerstrasse* we were under rigid surveillance, guards in their warm wool capes marching constantly up and down. It was the same in the center room of the barracks: half a dozen guards or camp police always present. Yet, in the large dormitory room there was almost no supervision at all. We did not understand it.[1]

Corrie and Betsie later discovered the reason no guards were in their room: The guards were afraid of contracting fleas! God had used the tiny fleas to protect His bold women from strong, intimidating enemy guards. How marvelous are God's ways!

Boldness is God's weapon for intimidating the devil. Some of the descriptions the dictionary uses in defining "bold" are "showing a readiness to take risks or face danger; daring; fearless; forceful in expression."[2] Corrie and Betsie certainly fit those descriptions!

ADVANCEMENT IN THE LORD'S PURPOSES

Christians often think they should never be bold. Sometimes they are instructed to relinquish all rights and forgive whoever wrongs them. There is truth in these teachings: However, we must also be discerning as to the tactics of the enemy who does not want us to advance in the Lord's purposes. He wants to keep us crouched in fear, intimidation and insecurity. God's Word declares that fear and intimidation are not from the Lord:

> For God has not given us a spirit of timidity, but of power and love and discipline (2 Tim. 1:7).

Fear and timidity were strongholds in my life while I was growing up. I was afraid of everything! I had fears of heights, people and authority figures. You name it, I was afraid of it. I had convinced myself that some people were outgoing, and others were not. I was sure I had been created as a quiet, timid individual. It was not until I discovered truths in God's Word and received healing for past wounds that I was able to come out of fear and timidity. People today see the boldness in my life and are amazed that I could ever have been so fearful. What the Lord has done for me, He can do for you. God does not show partiality (see Acts 10:34).

God's will for our lives is that we possess a spirit of boldness. The New Testament book of Hebrews reveals the heart of God for us in coming into His presence. The atoning sacrifice of the blood of Jesus has made a way for believers to approach the Throne of God. We do not need to fear death. Our sins are forgiven. We have been washed clean. We have absolute confidence in our right to be in the Throne Room. Therefore, we can come before the Lord in a spirit of boldness without the fear of death.

Jesus paid the price; therefore, believers can come to Him with boldness and confidence:

> Having therefore, brethren, boldness to enter into the holiest by the blood of Jesus (Heb. 10:19, *KJV*).

The apostle Paul was filled with boldness. Although he suffered deeply throughout his ministry years, his times of imprisonment were turned into powerful victories for the gospel of Christ. Paul wrote to the Philippians that his difficult circumstances would not hinder the boldness of the Lord in his life:

> For I know that this shall turn to my salvation through your prayer, and the supply of the Spirit of Jesus Christ, according to my earnest expectation and my hope, that in nothing I shall be ashamed, but that with all boldness, as always, so now also Christ shall be magnified in my body, whether it be by life, or by death (Phil. 1:19-20, *KJV*).

HINDRANCES TO BOLDNESS

Several things can hinder the spirit of boldness from operating in any Christian's life.

Lack of Knowledge

Often believers are not taught to be bold. Somehow, in my mind, I thought boldness was not Christlike. If I wanted to be like Jesus, I had to be nice to people and keep my mouth shut. Bold people seemed arrogant and haughty. I was wrong because I was suffering from a lack of knowledge: "My people are destroyed for lack of knowledge" (Hos. 4:6).

Have you read the story of the man who had a large inheritance in the bank but died bankrupt because he was unaware of the money that belonged to him? Sometimes Christians are like that. Due to our lack of knowledge, our spiritual lives are bankrupt. The Bible is full of examples of godly men and women who exhibited great boldness without arrogance or haughtiness.

Past Wounds

Another hindrance to boldness is wounds from the past. We tend to link boldness to abusive authority figures we have known. As a result, when we need to address a person in authority, we shrink back. Fear and timidity rise up. Since God is an authority figure, we even shrink back from boldly approaching Him. Instead we come to Him in prayer as a beggar: "Please, Lord. I need You to answer this prayer. I know I am not worthy. I realize I am a sinner. You are holy and I am nothing. However, if You can see beyond my weaknesses, please grant me this request." Yes, we would be nothing without God and Jesus' act of love on the cross, but that does not mean we have to pray in the language of a beggar. Pleading, self-abasing and separating from the love of God are inherent in a beggar's prayers. Past wounds cause us to see ourselves this way and separate us from the unconditional love of God.

But there is a way for those wounds to be healed. When Jesus died on the cross, He bore our grief and sorrow (see Isa. 53:4). When we release our hurts and forgive those who have wounded us, we receive God's love. That love removes our fear, timidity and insecurity:

> Herein is our love made perfect, that we may have boldness in the day of judgment: because as he is, so are we in this world. There is no fear in love; but perfect love casteth out fear: because fear hath torment. He that feareth is not made perfect in love (1 John 4:17-18, *KJV*).

God's love sets us free and allows us to have boldness when we come before Him in prayer.

There is a proper protocol in the Throne Room of God. We do not come to Him as beggars. If my children crawled to me and begged me to do something, I would be saddened. How painful it would be for me to think that my children were fearful or intimidated when asking me to do something for them! I get great delight in knowing they can approach me in boldness, trusting me and knowing that I love them.

> *God's love sets us free and allows us to have boldness.*

A Humble Heart

False assumptions can also hinder boldness. I have already noted the wrong supposition that a bold person is arrogant and haughty. Many times we look at an outward manifestation and judge the heart of an individual. A humble heart is willing to stand up boldly for the Lord. By contrast, when in a protective mode, we tend to try not to offend anyone or cause problems. Frequently, we are not doing this for the Lord's purpose but merely to defend our own reputation. Ask the Lord to search your heart—see if your timidity is actually a shield of self-protection:

> Search me, O God, and know my heart; try me and know my anxious thoughts; and see if there be any hurtful way in me, and lead me in the everlasting way (Ps. 139:23-24).

Control

Another false assumption is that boldness is linked with control. Not wanting to control, we tend to decline to be bold. But we need to see that control is neither evil nor good. It depends on what we do with it.

Good control is necessary for order on Earth. Dams are used to control water so that the surrounding area is protected from a destroying flood. Pest control is used to prevent disease and sickness. Speed limits are used to control dangerous driving that can cause death. All of these controls are used for good purposes.

Evil control involves exerting power over the will of other people. Some religious leaders use fear to control their followers, sometimes threatening them with punishment and even death if they leave the leader's particular religious system. The boldness of the Lord should never be used for evil purposes—specifically not to control others.

Some groups such as the Mafia, racial supremacists and occult factions also use control for wrong purposes. Those kinds of control are from the enemy and need to be resisted.

Intimidation

The spirit of intimidation seems to be a major hindrance to boldness in the lives of many Christians. The terrorist attacks in New York and Washington, D.C., on September 11, 2001, were an endeavor to intimidate Americans. For months afterwards many people refused to fly because they were terrified. The airline industry and the entire American economy have been affected by the attacks. Radical enemies of Christians and Jews tried to hinder those they consider infidels (people who do not follow Islam).

Moses was a man who had to overcome a spirit of intimidation. He knew he was destined to be a deliverer of God's people. After witnessing a fight between an Egyptian and a Hebrew, Moses killed the Egyptian. The next day he watched two Hebrew men fighting each other. After he boldly reprimanded them for fighting, one of the Hebrew men rebuked Moses, seeking to intimidate him:

He said, "Who made you a prince or a judge over us? Are you intending to kill me as you killed the Egyptian?" Then Moses was afraid and said, "Surely the matter has become known" (Exod. 2:14).

At that time Moses did not possess the inner strength for the authority and boldness God wanted him to have. As a result he ran from the situation. Years later Moses received a powerful call from God at the burning bush (see Exod. 3).

With this vision came a new level of authority for Moses. This authority, however, was rejected by Miriam and Aaron after Moses led Israel out of Egypt:

And they said, "Has the LORD indeed spoken only through Moses? Has He not spoken through us as well?" And the LORD heard it (Num. 12:2).

This time Moses was not touched by human words. He had reached a place where he was no longer intimidated by slander. When we are overwhelmed and intimidated by derogatory comments, we are not ready for the level of authority God wants us to have. We must deal with intimidation and realize that the Lord has heard the words and will be our defense.

Moses was not the only person in the Bible whom the enemy tried to intimidate. Ezra led a delegation of people out of Babylonian captivity. After these people returned to Jerusalem to rebuild the Temple, the enemy tried to discourage them. The children of Israel were considered infidels. Does that sound familiar? The terrorist attacks in America were the same type of attacks that occurred in the time of Ezra. A spirit of intimidation came against them to try to stop them from advancing and bringing forth restoration.

Years later Nehemiah returned to Jerusalem to help restore the city walls. Due to war, the walls were down and the gates had been burned. After Nehemiah encouraged the citizens to rebuild the walls, enemies sought to intimidate them and halt the work. Sanballat and Tobiah saw the bold exploits of the people in Jerusalem and did everything possible to stop them from advancing in God's purposes:

> *Overcoming intimidation is necessary for releasing a new level of authority in intercession.*

Now it came about that when Sanballat heard that we were rebuilding the wall, he became furious and very angry and mocked the Jews. He spoke in the presence of his brothers and the wealthy men of Samaria and said, "What are these feeble Jews doing? Are they going to restore it for themselves? Can they offer sacrifices? Can they finish in a day? Can they revive the stones from the dusty rubble even the burned ones?"

Now Tobiah the Ammonite was near him and he said, "Even what they are building—if a fox should jump on it, he would break their stone wall down!" (Neh. 4:1-3).

The enemy uses this same strategy today. We must resist the spirit of intimidation when it comes to mock us. Satan, the accuser of the brethren, makes accusations against us day and night (see Rev. 12:10). Some of the enemy's taunts may sound like this:

- "Who do you think you are?"
- "What makes you think you can do this?"
- "How do you know that you are able to hear from God?"

All of these questions are intimidations from the enemy designed to prevent us from advancing in releasing God's will on Earth through powerful, bold intercession. Overcoming intimidation is necessary for releasing a new level of authority in intercession.

MODELS OF BOLDNESS

Boldness is a characteristic seen in the life of the apostles. Peter and John exhibited it at the gate Beautiful (see Acts 3). Before the lame man was healed, they exhorted him, "Look at us!" (v. 4). They were bold in letting the man know that they did not have what he was asking for—money. However, they had what he needed—authority to heal! The religious leaders of the day saw the apostles' boldness and were fearful of losing their influence with the people, so they prevented Peter and John from speaking by arresting them and having them thrown in jail.

However, after their release, Peter and John continued to be bold and proclaim the good news of Jesus—boldness for the apostles meant continuing to preach the gospel despite arrests and death threats. The people continued to glorify the Lord for all that had happened:

> Now when they saw the boldness and unfettered elo-
> quence of Peter and John and perceived that they were
> unlearned and untrained in the schools [common men
> with no educational advantages], they marveled; and they
> recognized that they had been with Jesus (Acts 4:13, AMP).

Why do we need boldness in intercession? Boldness releases the authority of the Lord. Authority puts a demand on the release of God's will on Earth. We are not demanding that God release His will; He continually wants His will to be manifest on Earth. We are demanding that the enemy and all hindrances be blocked, so the will of God comes forth. The spirit of boldness releases a courageous level of authority.

The Power of Expectancy

What do we need to release the spirit of boldness? Expectancy! Expectancy releases the will of God from the heavenly store-room. Young David in the Bible expected God to give him victory over the giant Goliath. Saul's army was intimidated by Goliath's taunts. Yet David had great expectancy that the Lord would cause His will to manifest itself on Earth. David operated in boldness and expectancy in the face of Goliath's intimidation:

> Your servant has killed both the lion and the bear; and this uncircumcised Philistine will be like one of them, since he has taunted the armies of the living God (1 Sam. 17:36).

God saw David's expectation and caused him to defeat the enemy that had put fear into the hearts of Saul's army.

> The wicked flee when no one is pursuing, but the righteous are bold as a lion (Prov. 28:1).

David had a cause that released boldness and expectancy. His cause was the advancing of God's purpose and God's name on Earth. Our cause should be the same today!

The Appearance of Signs and Wonders

The apostles of the Early Church also resisted the taunts of the enemy and the religious leaders. Their prayers included requests for a spirit of boldness to operate in their lives:

> And now, Lord, behold their threatenings: and grant unto thy servants, that with all boldness they may speak

thy word, by stretching forth thine hand to heal; and that signs and wonders may be done by the name of thy holy child Jesus. And when they had prayed, the place was shaken where they were assembled together; and they were all filled with the Holy Ghost, and they spake the word of God with boldness (Acts 4:29-31, *KJV*).

After the apostles' prayed, there was an earthquake. The building shook and an outpouring of the Holy Spirit occurred. The apostles then went forth in great boldness, while preaching the Word with signs, wonders and miracles following them. God's will was manifest on Earth as the apostles operated in a spirit of boldness.

We, as believers today, can operate the same way. The results will be the same. Signs, wonders, miracles and the release of God's will into this world will be revealed and manifest!

You may want to pray the following prayer:

Father, I come to You today with a heart of expectancy. I confess that I have been fearful and subject to intimidation. I ask You to forgive me for wanting to protect my reputation more than the desire to advance Your kingdom. I forgive abusive authority figures and others who have intimidated me in the past. Thank You for purchasing my freedom from fear and timidity on the Cross. Thank You for giving me Your perfect love, which casts out all my fear. Fill me with a spirit of boldness. Use me to boldly proclaim Your will. I love You, Lord. May Your will be manifest on Earth, even as it is in heaven. In Jesus' name I pray. Amen.

Notes
1. Corrie ten Boom and John and Elizabeth Sherrill, *Hiding Place* (Minneapolis, MN: World Wide Publications, 1971), pp. 201-202.
2. *Webster's New World College Dictionary*, 4th ed., s.v. "bold."

CHAPTER 5

A NEW LEVEL
OF FAITH

Each year my husband and I vacation with two other couples. We love to get away and just relax together as friends. Usually we spend one night watching a movie. I would rather read a book, so it is difficult to find a movie that I like. On one of these vacations, we walked into the video-rental store in anticipation of which movie might hold my interest.

As we scanned the shelves for just the right movie, I spotted something. In front of me was a cover that looked interesting. The title—*The Inn of the Sixth Happiness*—jumped out. A corporate decision was quickly made: We had found our movie.

That night we watched it together. The story unfolded about a young woman with a burning passion to go to China as a missionary. People in her religious hierarchy told her she could not go because she was a single woman. That was the wrong thing to tell Gladys Aylward! She was determined to go.

Each week Miss Aylward worked and put part of her earnings into a bank account. After a period of time, there was enough money in the account to purchase a one-way ticket to China. The tremendous level of faith in this lady was inspiring. God used her in a powerful way to help change a society. She not only had faith to overcome the hindrance of religious leaders opposed to her calling, but she also had faith to overcome every obstacle while on the mission field.

- How do some people reach such great levels of faith?
- Is this kind of faith available for those who never go to a foreign mission field?
- What can we do to cause our faith to grow?
- Why is this level of faith necessary in intercession?

A Necessary Principle

From Genesis to Revelation, the Bible teaches us about faith. Even with so much written about faith, many Christians do not understand it. The dictionary gives several definitions of the word: "unquestioning belief that does not require proof or evidence; unquestioning belief in God, religious tenets, etc.; anything believed; complete trust, confidence, or reliance."[1] Faith then is a necessary principle of spiritual life.

Hebrews gives not only a definition of faith but also a description of its effect:

> Now faith is the assurance (the confirmation, the title deed) of the things [we] hope for, being the proof of things [we] do not see and the conviction of their reality [faith perceiving as real fact what is not revealed to the

senses]. For by [faith—trust and holy fervor born of faith] the men of old had divine testimony borne to them and obtained a good report (Heb. 11:1-2, *AMP*).

Mighty men and women of God are written about in Hebrews. These people did not just give mental assent to the need for faith; their lives were also testimonies to a faith that was vital and active. It was the force that motivated them in all they did. Their faith demanded a better tomorrow than what they were currently experiencing.

One of the mighty men mentioned in the Bible is Noah, a man of outstanding faith. Noah was willing to obey God without a visible manifestation of God's promise. He built an ark to prepare for a flood, even though there had never been 40 days of rain. He was confident that God would do what He said He would do. Although Noah met much opposition as he prepared the ark, he persisted. He believed God would do the impossible:

[Prompted] by faith Noah, being forewarned by God concerning events of which as yet there was no visible sign, took heed and diligently and reverently constructed and prepared an ark for the deliverance of his own family. By this [his faith which relied on God] he passed judgment and sentence on the world's unbelief and became an heir and possessor of righteousness (that relation of being right into which God puts the person who has faith) (Heb. 11:7, *AMP*).

CALLED TO THE IMPOSSIBLE

Faith never operates in the realm of the possible. It seems that the Lord always asks me to do that which I cannot do. Have you noticed He does the same thing with you? When He called me to preach His Word, I knew that was impossible. If I could not speak to three people without my voice closing off, how could I preach to many? But God did the impossible! I had to reach a place where I believed Him more than my circumstances. If I would do what he asked me to do, He would perform the miracle.

Faith never operates in the realm of the possible.

God receives great glory when He performs that which is humanly impossible. Faith begins where our power ends. (God receives glory through our faith in Him.) Faith brings the Lord onto the scene and causes the impossible to become possible. With God there are no impossibilities!

For each of us a time comes when we must make a decision. We must decide if we are going to have faith in what God has said, in spite of our circumstances. We make this choice in intercession. Will we be God's mouthpieces to speak His Word, declare His purposes and release His bold plan into the world—or will we shrink back in unbelief?

An Imperative Assignment

Like Noah, Abraham was also a man of excellent faith. His faith was manifest in his obedience. Sometimes faith requires a person to do things that seem unreasonable. Faith deals with the supernatural and the divine. Faith to obey God does not always seem reasonable. Abraham was called to leave his homeland, not knowing where he was going. The Lord commanded him, and by faith he was to journey into a new place. To the natural mind, that kind of action is unreasonable. Conversely, to the mind of faith, obeying the Lord is very reasonable. It is the most sensible, sane, rational thing a person can do. Obeying the Lord and speaking His words and plans by faith are imperative assignments for intercessors.

As I noted in chapter 2, I made several trips to Russia during the 1990s, planting churches and holding retreats for pastors. During one retreat I spoke a word from the Lord over a young pastor: "God is going to give you a building for your church." Another leader attending the meeting later told me he had listened with much unbelief. After all, the country was impoverished. The pastor who received the word had no means to obtain a building. Furthermore, the government and religious system in the country would oppose the pastor's having a building. Yet one year later the pastor was given a building! God had spoken, and the impossible became possible.

EXERCISING FAITH

Intercessors are being called to a new level of faith for the new season in which we now live. The faith we operated in during the last season will not be sufficient for the task the Lord has given to us for this season. Our faith should always be growing. Intercessors are to go from one level of faith to another (see Rom. 1:17).

There are things we can do to help our faith grow. Faith is like a muscle that can be strengthened. If we do not use a muscle, it becomes weak and flabby. However, if we exercise the muscle, it becomes stronger and is capable of doing more than it did before exercising.

A Hope Before Us

One of the ways we exercise our faith is by keeping our hope before us. Athletes have a goal that cheers them on. They will do whatever it takes to cross the goal line and win the victory. When they get tired, when the victory seems out of reach, athletes will submit to whatever training is required in order to win. The prize is always before them, calling them forth.

People who are satisfied with the routine of daily living will never be among the ranks of the winners. They will simply drift through life, enduring whatever comes their way. They will not do what it takes to break out of the ordinary and taste the extraordinary.

An old adage declares, A champion does not become a champion in the ring—he is simply recognized there. How true that is! The men and women of God listed in Hebrews did not become champions of faith in a moment. They exercised their faith against all odds and were later recognized as giants in the ring of faith. It took years of exercising to reach that point. They refused to settle for the ordinary. They kept the hope of God's promise before them as they submitted to whatever came their way.

Perseverance

Another way we can exercise our faith is through perseverance. Often we find people who start well. They can do whatever it takes to run the race in the beginning. From time to time, they may even experience great victories. The challenge comes in continuing to be faithful to the end and persevering at all times:

> Yet those who wait for the LORD will gain new strength; they will mount up with wings like eagles, they will run and not get tired, they will walk and not become weary (Isa. 40:31).

Some are able to mount up like eagles from time to time. A certain level of faith is required for mounting up. However, not all will run without becoming weary or walk the walk of faith without fainting. Faith must be exercised to reach this capacity.

Vision for the End
The next way we are able to exercise our faith is to have vision for the end:

> For the vision is yet for the appointed time; it hastens toward the goal and it will not fail. Though it tarries, wait for it; for it will certainly come, it will not delay (Hab. 2:3).

Intercessors must always have vision for the end. They must hold onto the words they have prayed and released. The victory belongs to those who do not quit before the manifestation of God's promise. His anointed words released through powerful intercession will cause His will to manifest on Earth. Remember the vision for the end and wait for the promise. It is only a matter of time. It will surely come.

BENEFITS OF GROWING IN FAITH

Growing in our faith will bring great benefits to each of us and to others.

Favor with God
The first benefit of growing in our faith is that it gains favor with God:

> And without faith it is impossible to please Him, for he who comes to God must believe that He is and that He is a rewarder of those who seek Him (Heb. 11:6).

The Lord rewards lives of faith. Miraculous workings of God's power are evident in the lives of those who have faith for a supernatural release of God's resources from heaven.

Moses lived in Egypt under the rule of a demonized the pharaoh, but he refused to be part of the ungodly political system there. Although he had grown up under the Egyptian political system, he knew he was an Israelite, not an Egyptian; therefore, he continued to believe that God would reward his faith (see Heb. 11:24-26).

Destruction of Satan's Strongholds

God rewards people of faith with a closer walk with Him. He also rewards them with the ability to break strongholds of the enemy. Pharaoh looked impossible to defeat. In spite of that, Moses continued to endure adversity, so he could gain the prize. How was he able to do this?

> By faith [Moses] left Egypt, not fearing the wrath of the king; for he endured, as seeing Him who is unseen (Heb. 11:27).

Rather than looking at the face of his enemy, Moses chose to see the King who is invisible. The invisible was more real to Moses than the visible. That is a reality of faith! Moses acted in faith so that a nation could be delivered:

> By faith he kept the Passover and the sprinkling of the blood, so that he who destroyed the firstborn would not touch them. By faith they passed through the Red Sea as though they were passing through dry land; and the Egyptians, when they attempted it, were drowned (Heb. 11:28-29).

Blood spread on a doorpost and a stick held in the air do not look like weapons that could break the power of the enemy— unless they are done as acts of faith. Moses obeyed God's words through faith and saw the miracles follow.

We do not have to do wild things to prove to God that we have faith. He sees our hearts. We cannot work up faith; we cannot manufacture it. Either we have it, or we do not. It is a gift, and it can be multiplied as we exercise the faith we already have.

Obtaining the Promise
Another benefit of faith is that we obtain the promise of the Lord:

> And what more shall I say? For time will fail me if I tell of Gideon, Barak, Samson, Jephthah, of David and Samuel and the prophets, who by faith conquered kingdoms, performed acts of righteousness, obtained promises, shut the mouths of lions, quenched the power of fire, escaped the edge of the sword, from weakness were made strong, became mighty in war, put foreign armies to flight (Heb. 11:32-34).

In Old Testament times, many men and women had nothing to hold on to but the promises of God. The promises had no visible evidence that they would be fulfilled; rather, they clearly were for the future. Therefore, the people of God acted as if the promises had already been made manifest. They believed God, whether their eyes saw the promise or not. They took Him at His word and lived their lives confident of His reward.

Intercessors often have nothing to hold on to but the Word of God. Some situations look as if they will never change. Still, those whose faith has been stretched will be confident of the release of God's will into the situations about which they are praying. Faith-filled words released into the world will bring favor with God, destroy the power of the enemy and obtain the promises of the Lord.

Mountain-Moving Faith

The faith that has been described thus far is mountain-moving faith:

> Truly I say to you, whoever says to this mountain, "Be taken up and cast into the sea," and does not doubt in his heart, but believes that what he says is going to happen, it will be granted him. Therefore I say to you, all things for which you pray and ask, believe that you have received them, and they will be granted you (Mark 11:23-24).

Mountains in the Bible sometimes represent difficulty or resistance to the will of God. Intercessors have the authority to speak to the resistance and command it to be removed. Notice that the person is not told to speak to God. When we understand that we are the voice of the Lord on Earth, we can put faith behind our words, as I wrote about in my book *Prophetic Intercession*:

> *When we understand that we are the voice of the Lord on Earth, we can put faith behind our words.*

The voice of the Lord causes the enemy to be afraid. It causes him to be so terrified he will tremble with pain. God's voice also causes the words spoken to produce and bring forth. His voice births the fruit of our labors. I am convinced that if we could see into the realm of the spirit, we would pray more. Often, we pray, but because we don't see an immediate answer, we think nothing has happened. Remember it took 21 days for the answer to come to Daniel (see Dan. 10:12-13). Sometimes it will take

even more time before we see the results of our intercession.[2]

Our words can move aside the resistance of the enemy. Our
faith-filled words have the authority to create the will of God out
of nothing. It is the same principle that was operating at the
time of creation:

> By faith we understand that the worlds were prepared by
> the word of God, so that what is seen was not made out
> of things which are visible (Heb. 11:3).

We speak the words of God, activating them by faith and cre-
ating His will on Earth out of nothing. His voice through intercessors commands a release of *something* out of *nothing*!

In the beginning, God spoke and caused light to be released:

> Then God said, "Let there be light"; and there was light
> (Gen. 1:3).

Darkness could not resist the light. Light had to be! When God
spoke His will for Earth, His will had to manifest itself. When
intercessors operate in the same kind of God-driven faith, the will
of God is released on Earth. The mountain has to move. The resistance to God's will must stop. The promises of God shall come!

Ask the Lord to stretch your faith as you pray the following
prayer:

> *Father, I recognize I need my faith to increase for this new sea-*
> *son in my life. I do believe. Help my unbelief! By the power of*
> *Your Holy Spirit, remind me to keep my eyes on Him, who is*
> *unseen. I resist looking at natural circumstances. I choose to see*
> *the end of the promise. Let my words always be filled with faith*

so that I may please You and receive the reward. Cause the words of my mouth to create Your will on the earth. Use them to create the visible manifestation of Your promises on Earth out of the unseen. Thank You for hearing and answering my prayer. In Jesus' name. Amen.

Notes

1. *Webster's New World College Dictionary*, 4th ed., s.v. "faith."
2. Barbara Wentroble, *Prophetic Intercession* (Ventura, CA: Renew Books, 1999), p. 79.

CHAPTER 6

INDIVIDUAL AUTHORITY

"I do it myself!"

My daughter Lori was only two and a half years old, but she was trying to act much older by declaring her independence. If anyone attempted to help feed her, put her clothes on or do most anything for her, she resisted. She wanted to do it herself! To say she was independent would be an understatement. Lori liked the freedom she experienced when she accomplished feats. She loved to feel she had a measure of authority to rule her life.

Those first few years of Lori's life were challenging. My husband, Dale, and I sought to steer our daughter's desire to control her own life in the right direction. We knew that God places traits like these in children for good purposes, but we also knew that sometimes the enemy seeks to redirect those traits in wrong directions. We are blessed that Lori now uses this God-given strength for the Lord's purposes in her life. It has protected her during the growing-up years and now serves to point her toward the Lord's plan.

KNOW MANKIND'S HEAVENLY MANDATE

The Lord has given each of us authority. We must be able to properly exercise that authority in our own lives before we can be released to exercise it in a wider sphere.

As we have seen in Genesis 1:26-28, mankind was originally created by God to exercise authority on Earth. Mankind was made in God's image and given authority on Earth as God's representative. Mankind's purpose was to use this delegated authority to extend the dominion of the Lord until Earth was filled with God's glory.

Mankind, however, failed to fulfill its heavenly mandate. We believed the lies of Satan more than the truth of God. The enemy tempted the woman with the forbidden fruit from the tree in the middle of the Garden:

> The serpent said to the woman, "You surely will not die!
> For God knows that in the day you eat from it your eyes
> will be opened, and you will be like God, knowing good
> and evil" (Gen. 3:4-5).

When Eve initially resisted the temptation, Satan lied and deceived her. She and Adam then ate the fruit. This is what is called the Fall. As a result of the Fall, sin entered the picture and man lost dominion on Earth. Man also lost dominion over himself and no longer had the authority to release God's glory on Earth.

Restore What Was Lost

All of this did not change God's mind concerning His plan for mankind. In the fullness of time God sent His own Son to restore all that had been lost due to sin:

> And the Word became flesh, and dwelt among us, and we saw His glory, glory as of the only begotten from the Father, full of grace and truth (John 1:14).

For those of us who are Christians, God has restored authority to rule on Earth. As the process of transformation is embraced in each believer's life, God's glory is manifest:

> Therefore I urge you, brethren, by the mercies of God, to present your bodies a living and holy sacrifice, acceptable to God, which is your spiritual service of worship. And do not be conformed to this world, but be transformed by the renewing of your mind, so that you may prove what the will of God is, that which is good and acceptable and perfect (Rom. 12:1-2).

The key then to walking a life of victory is to renew the mind according to the Word of God. We must say what God's Word says about us rather than what our emotions tell us. He has made us new creations. We are not our former selves. We are becoming the people He originally created us to be.

Find a New Focus

Too many Christians try to live victorious lives by constantly focusing on crucifying the flesh, instead of repenting and turning away from the things of the flesh. They are constantly attempting to deal a deathblow to the old Adamic nature, rather than manifesting the Christ-life on Earth. Remember when a teacher would have a talkative student stay after school? The student would be required to write 100 times on the chalkboard "I will not talk in class." What were the results? The next day the same student would talk in class. Focusing on the negative does not work. Victory is found through concentration on the positive nature of Jesus within us:

> To whom God willed to make known what is the riches of the glory of this mystery among the Gentiles, which is Christ in you, the hope of glory (Col. 1:27).

Failure to properly rule our own lives is like living in an unprotected city without walls:

> Like a city that is broken into and without walls is a man who has no control over his spirit (Prov. 25:28).

The Bible often notes walled cities. Many of these walls were constructed of mud or clay mixed with reeds and hardened in the sun. The walls around the cities were used for protection and safety from enemies. Anytime there was a breach in the walls, the consequences were serious.

In the same way, whenever we do not bring our own spirit and emotions under the control of the Holy Spirit, there are serious consequences. We not only lose our ability to exercise authority on Earth, but we also make way for the enemy in our lives. Consequently, we do not manifest God's glory. However, the Lord has provided a way for us to defeat the old Adamic nature through the power of the Holy Spirit. I love what Doug Fortune writes in his book *Apostolic Reformation: In His Image*:

Well, Christ is residing IN YOU, so you're going about your day and someone is offensive toward you . . . the "man of sin" is revealed in you, the First Adam-nature rises up . . . THIS is when Christ must slay him with the Spirit of His mouth! So you say (remember, He is IN YOU), "That feeling is a LIE from my SOUL, I have the compassion of Christ for this one who is being offensive." You respond from your SPIRIT, a higher dimension, NOT from the SOUL realm in which the principalities and powers have authority . . . you can only defeat principalities and powers by operating from a higher realm. You see, the proper response is already WITHIN you because CHRIST is IN YOU, and as the "man of sin," the First Adam nature that is lodged in your mind is slain, it is replaced with the MIND of Christ (1 Cor. 2:16). This is what Rom. 12:2 refers to as the renewing of your mind.

Your focus must NOT be on overcoming the sin-nature of your SOUL, your focus must be on Christ IN YOU who has ALREADY overcome the sin-nature. It's not a matter of training your Adam-nature to act better, it is a matter of a NEW nature, the nature of Christ which is IN YOUR SPIRIT, because " . . . he who is joined to the Lord becomes ONE SPIRIT with Him" (1 Cor. 6:17). It is a matter of first REALIZING that the perfection of Christ is IN YOU, no matter what your mind, will and emotions tell you.[1]

Learn to Rest

Too often Christians are taught religious practices that keep the focus on battling the old, Adamic sin nature. The result is that we become tired and weary from the struggle. A great deal of negative energy is required when we are always trying to be good enough. Hebrews teaches that the Word divides between the spirit and the soul (see 4:12). The Word of God is like a sword. It will cut off every sinful thought and intent of the heart. The Word will bring us to a place of rest—the Lord promises this for His people:

> Therefore, let us fear if, while a promise remains of entering His rest, any one of you may seem to have come short of it (Heb. 4:1).

Sometimes we equate rest with inactivity. This is not what the Lord is talking about. He is speaking of receiving by faith what He has done for us. We cease our labors of trying to crucify the old nature. We rest in what Jesus did for us through His death, burial and resurrection. No longer do we walk in unbelief. We embrace a revelation of the finished work of the Cross.

A yielding to the Christ nature within us leads to a place of rest. As God rested when His work of creation was finished, we also must rest in what Jesus did in us when we became new creations. As we allow Jesus (the Word) to live His life through us, we become the expression of Him on Earth. His glory now fills us and causes us to advance the kingdom of God. We receive a new level of authority over the plans of the enemy.

Yield to His Nature

The authority of God resides in His glory. The glory of God is the fire of God. The *shekinah* presence of God manifests itself through our lives. His glory in us gives us a higher level of authority to deal with the powers of darkness. Ana Mendez writes of this glory in her book *Shaking the Heavens*:

> It is the same fire that shone in the burning bush that attracted Moses' attention in the wilderness. There was

no trial, and there was no shame for Moses; the fire was the glorious manifestation that was going to raise him up as Israel's deliverer, the revelation of the living God that would take him before Pharaoh. It was the strength, the *dunamis* of God the all power-ful with which Moses would con-front the empire of darkness. It was the fullness of the Spirit in its plenitude that would enable him to stand before the proud and feared Egyptian empire and say, "Pharoah, thus says the Lord, . . . *Let My people go"* (Exod. 5:1, *AMP*, emphasis added).

> *God's glory in us gives us a higher level of authority to deal with the powers of darkness.*

This same fire is descending today upon the Church, raising up men and women anointed with the authority of God to stand before the devil. They will become true warriors in prayer, soldiers in God's army capable of releasing God's authoritative Word, storming the gates of hell and ordering the powers and principalities, saying "In the Name of Jesus, let God's people go!"[2]

Repent

How then do we yield to the Christ nature within us? First, we must repent for anything we have done that does not line up with the nature of Christ. I am not talking about introspection. Introspection causes us to look at ourselves rather than at the Lord. If we look to the Lord, He will reveal any area that needs repentance:

> Search me, O God, and know my heart; try me and know my anxious thoughts; and see if there be any hurtful way

in me, and lead me in the everlasting way (Ps. 139:23-24).

It is important that rather than digging around ourselves, we allow the Holy Spirit to search our hearts and look for sin. God will reveal what needs correcting.

Whenever the Holy Spirit puts a spotlight on a wrong thought or action, we simply need to repent—that is all. Repentance means *a change of mind and direction*. It is not a feeling; it is an action. Godly sorrow causes us to think and act like the Lord:

> I now rejoice, not that you were made sorrowful, but that you were made sorrowful to the point of repentance; for you were made sorrowful according to the will of God, so that you might not suffer loss in anything through us. For the sorrow that is according to the will of God produces a repentance without regret, leading to salvation, but the sorrow of the world produces death (2 Cor. 7:9-10).

From time to time we all will find ourselves in one situation or another that we do not like. Often when this happens, we seek to change our job, spouse, church or counselor. In other words, we look for any opportunity to change the circumstances of our life rather than stopping to realize that maybe the Lord wants to get us to operate from our spirit, not our soulish nature. Getting out of the situation is not always the answer. Too often we fail to see what the Lord is doing in our lives at a particular moment. (Of course, there are some situations, such as abusive relationships, that people must escape.)

Sometimes the enemy is not the devil, other people or God. The enemy is me!

Often when people run from a situation, a pattern begins to form in their lives. From then on, whenever situations become uncomfortable, they run. The problem is that they keep going around the same mountain and get nowhere. Remember the old saying, I have found the enemy, and it is me? How true that is. Sometimes the enemy is not the devil, it is not other people, nor is it God. The enemy is me! I must stop fighting the people and circumstances the Lord puts in my life. When we find the presence of the Lord in every situation, we will yield to the Lord, not to emotions.

Take Every Thought Captive
We can also yield to the Lord by taking every thought captive:

> We are destroying speculations and every lofty thing raised up against the knowledge of God, and we are taking every thought captive to the obedience of Christ (2 Cor. 10:5).

We must reject the old feeling, not fight with it. As long as we focus on resisting emotions such as rejection, abandonment, unworthiness and anger, we give strength and life to them. Whatever we nourish will live. However, if we starve something, it will die. As long as a basketball player dribbles the ball, it will keep bouncing. When the player stops dribbling, the ball will eventually roll away and stop. Old emotions are the same way. When we stop focusing on them, they will eventually cease. Therefore, we starve the old feelings and, instead, feed our thoughts with words of God's truth. We are then able to go on in life, ignoring and not giving life to contrary thoughts.

Respond with Forgiveness
A vital step in being able to yield to the Christ nature within us is to respond to offenses and hurts with forgiveness. I once heard

someone say, "It's easy to forgive until you have something to forgive." How true that is! However, God has called us to walk in forgiveness so that we may also receive forgiveness.

> For if you forgive others for their transgressions, your heavenly Father will also forgive you (Matt. 6:14).

Choosing to forgive someone does not necessarily mean that person was right. It simply means we have released him or her into the hands of the Lord. We are then free to go on in life without bitterness or anger. How wonderful to be free from old hurts that can keep us locked in the past! Rather than responding out of bitterness and anger, we respond out of the nature of Jesus. When He hung on the cross, Jesus responded to His enemies through forgiveness:

> But Jesus was saying, "Father, forgive them; for they do not know what they are doing" (Luke 23:34).

Stick with It

Perseverance is needed as we learn to yield to the Christ nature within us. Too many times people give up just before the victory. The Lord is watching over us and has promised rewards to the overcomer (see Rev. 2:7). Since we are following Jesus, we are on the winning side. Therefore, we continue to persevere until we see the full manifestation of all He has promised for us.

Since we are following Jesus, we are on the winning side.

Yielding to the Christ nature within us gives us authority to rule over our lives. Walking in that authority then positions us for authority to be extended into greater spheres of responsibility. As we learn to enjoy our journey with the Lord, He gives us the grace we need along the way.

Take a Humor Break

I have learned to laugh at my mistakes. This is one act that helps me press on to victory. I used to get stressed out whenever I did something wrong. One day the Lord spoke to my heart and said, "Barbara, I am bigger than your mistakes." That word from the Lord changed my life! I realized He did not fall off His throne and did not stop this planet from spinning because I made a mistake. He knew all along that I was not perfect. How amazing that He uses imperfect vessels to get the job done!

I do not give the enemy credit for anything in my life. Jesus has won every victory. In fact, He took every rubbish pile of my life and turned it into fertilizer to help me grow into the person I am becoming. He will do the same for you. So do yourself a favor: Take a humor break! You deserve it.

Heavenly Father, I desire to have my mind renewed.
I believe Your Word is truth. I choose to believe what Your
Word says about me rather than what the lies of the enemy
and the lies of my flesh tell me. I choose to focus on the Christ
nature within me rather than my old Adamic nature. Thank
You for making me a new creation.
Empower me, Lord, to rule over my emotions. I give the
Holy Spirit freedom to lead me so that I won't continue to be
led by my feelings. I rest in all You have done for me.
I forgive every person and every situation that has brought
hurt or pain into my life. Forgive me for any bitterness or
resentment that is in my heart.
Thank You for bringing me to a place of rest.

Teach me how to laugh at my mistakes. I am not perfect,
but You are. Thank You that I now receive a new authority
to rule over my emotions. Be glorified in my life.
In Jesus' name. Amen.

Notes

1. Doug Fortune, *Apostolic Reformation: In His Image* (McPherson, KS: Trumpet Call Publishing, 2001), p. 19.
2. Ana Mendez, *Shaking the Heavens* (Ventura, CA: Renew Books, 2000), pp. 33-34.

CHAPTER 7

CORPORATE
AUTHORITY

Doris and Peter Wagner have roots as dairy farmers in upper New York State. Attending livestock shows and watching the draft horse competitions are two of their lifelong loves. Although I know nothing about horse shows, I enjoy listening to Peter's stories. He sometimes tells of the phenomenal strength produced by hitching two horses together. He wrote about this power in his book *Apostles and Prophets*.

> We love to see those magnificent Percherons and Clydesdales and Belgians and Shires working together as teams. The climax of all events is the horse pull, in which a team of two horses weighing a combined 4,500 pounds often pulls 14,000 pounds of concrete blocks on a flat

sled. I remember one county fair that featured individual horse pulls. The winner pulled 5,000 pounds and the runner up pulled 4,000 pounds. But hitched together, they pulled 13,000 pounds![1]

The principle is the same whether it is horses or people: More team members mean more power. This works in the Church, too. Greater feats are possible as members of the corporate Body of Christ unite for rapid increase—we can do more as a group than we can as individuals. Rather than the results being *added* together, they are *multiplied* through a corporate effort! The Bible confirms this principle:

How could one chase a thousand, and two put ten thousand to flight . . . ? (Deut. 32:30).

An exponential increase resides in the power and authority of a corporate people to push back the forces of evil.

Often we speak of corporate America or of an individual corporation. The dictionary defines the word "corporate" as "united, combined; shared by all members of a unified group; common; joint."[2] The corporate Body of Christ simply refers to a united, combined or unified group of believers. This unification allows an exponential increase. This equation includes an unknown variable that rapidly increases the power. In the same way that a corporate team of horses is able to accomplish great things together, the corporate Body of Christ has greater authority to advance exponentially the will of God on Earth.

A LEVEL OF UNITY

One of the first things we learn about in the Bible is the level of unity in the Godhead. Although three forms of God are revealed to us as Father, Son and Holy Spirit, God is only one. Thus, the idea of corporateness began in heaven.

> Hear, O Israel! The LORD is our God, the LORD is one! (Deut. 6:4-5).

Judson Cornwall explains this in his book *Let Us Get Together*:

> The Trinity has never been three Gods, and we create much difficulty, not only conceptually but experientially, when we allow ourselves to separate the Father, the Son, and the Holy Spirit into three distinct persons who get along fine, but are three individuals. The Scripture teaches that there are not three Gods— "The Lord our God is one Lord"— there is but one God who has chosen to reveal Himself to us in three forms, and He has never been separated from Himself except for the brief interval at the cross when the Father turned His face from the Son. It was this separation between the Father and the Son that was the true agony of the cross; not the square Roman nails, not the aftermath of the whipping post, nor the poisonous crown of thorns, nor the disjointing of arms and legs as the cross was dropped into the ground. The physical agony of the crucifixion was nothing to be compared with the separation in the Godhead occasioned by Christ's vicarious bearing of our sins in His own body on that cross. It was both the first and the last separation that the Godhead will ever know.[3]

God desires for the unity that is in heaven to be manifest on Earth.

God desires for the unity that is in heaven to be manifest on Earth. God's love for corporateness is witnessed in His creation. God did not merely create one animal but many animals (see Gen. 1:20-25). He did not create only one tree but many trees (see vv. 11-12). He formed a river and caused it to become four rivers (see 2:10-14). After each act of creation God said, "It is good." Finally, He created man. When He saw that there was only one man, God said, "It is not good for the man to be alone" (2:18). It was the only time that God did not say His creation was good. He then created an equal out of man to come alongside him— woman (see 2:21-23). Together they would find satisfaction and fulfill the heart of God for Earth.

Mankind does not enjoy being alone. The worst thing that can happen to a prisoner is to be put in solitary confinement. People listen to radios or watch TV when they are alone. Many spend time in restaurants and bars to be around other people. Others obtain pets or read books to break the loneliness. A few years ago a fad for pet rocks became popular. Man was not made to be alone. In reality, man is desperate for companionship.

CORPORATE STRENGTH

God began His purposes with an individual man, but He consummates them with a corporate people. Intercessors unite in groups to pray for the Lord to cause our cities and territories to look like heaven. In the Bible, God gives us pictures of what heaven looks like. He does not give us these pictures so that we will be homesick and always wanting to leave Earth and go to heaven. He gives us pictures of heaven so that we will know what He wants Earth to look like. He also promises that a time will come when the glory of God will fill the earth (see Hab. 2:14).

In the Body of Christ, many individual believers are working hard to see the glory of God come to their cities or territories.

However, an individual person or church will not bring God's glory back to a city. The authority for restoration will come through a corporate people. This occurred in the Old Testament:

> When they came to the threshing floor of Chidon, Uzza put out his hand to hold the ark, because the oxen nearly upset it. The anger of the LORD burned against Uzza, so He struck him down because he put out his hand to the ark; and he died there before God (1 Chron. 13:9-10).

The Ark of God, which represented God's glorious presence, had rested in the house of Uzza's father, Abinidab, for 20 years. Priests were instructed by the Lord to carry the Ark using poles and rings. It was not to be carried on a man-made cart but on the shoulders of the priesthood (see Isa. 9:6). The administration for transporting the glory of God was disregarded in this instance. One man, Uzza, attempted to hold up the Ark when the oxen almost caused it to fall. Because of his disobedience to the Lord's instructions, Uzza died.

Too many individuals and single churches have attempted to bring the glory back to their cities. They are laboring to hold up the presence of the Lord without the assistance of other churches and believers. Some have experienced burnout or death to their vision and ministries. A corporate authority is needed to withstand the evil spiritual powers over certain cities and territories.

The children of Israel used this same rule for corporate authority as they crossed the Jordan River. A group of 12 spies was sent into the Promised Land to gain knowledge before the others entered. Later, a group of 12 priests stepped into the river, and the corporate spiritual authority upon them caused the water to part. After they crossed, 12 men took 12 stones from the river as a memorial to the faithfulness of God.

Twelve is a number that represents government.

Twelve denotes authority.

If the children of Israel were going to be able to cross over into their promise, they would need corporate authority over the hindrances. Their individual viewpoints were replaced with a corporate authority, so they were able to see cities and lands restored.

An example of corporate authority to change cities is found in the story of Jericho. Joshua led a corporate people into the Promised Land. He gave them the strategy for taking the city. When the Israelites obeyed the voice of Joshua and moved together as a corporate people, an authority in the Spirit was released. Using spiritual strategy through a corporate authority, they were able to take the city.

> So the people shouted, and priests blew the trumpets; and when the people heard the sound of the trumpet, the people shouted with a great shout and the wall fell down flat, so that the people went up into the city, every man straight ahead, and they took the city (Josh. 6:20).

Jesus-Type Ministry

Individual believers possess an authority in the Lord (see Luke 4:18). Jesus is quoted in John 14:12 as saying we have the authority to do the same works that He did. What are some of the works Jesus did?

- He healed the sick (see Mark 3:9-12; 1 Pet. 2:24).
- He raised the dead (see John 11:23).
- He set the captives free (see Isa. 61:1; Mark 3:14-15; Luke 11:20).
- He brought peace to troubled minds (see John 14:27).

Jesus spent three years teaching His disciples to minister as He did. He commissioned them after His resurrection, not to merely *talk* about the Kingdom, but to *demonstrate* it. The kingdom of God is demonstrated by releasing the spiritual authority necessary for performing signs, wonders and miracles.

> *The kingdom of God is demonstrated by releasing the spiritual authority necessary for performing signs, wonders and miracles.*

He who has believed and has been baptized shall be saved; but he who has disbelieved shall be condemned. These signs will accompany those who have believed: in My name they will cast out demons, they will speak with new tongues; they will pick up serpents, and if they drink any deadly poison, it will not hurt them; they will lay hands on the sick, and they will recover (Mark 16:16-18).

THE SPIRITUAL CLIMATE

Although individuals do have authority, they do not have the level of authority needed to pull down demonic strongholds and territorial spirits over cities and territories. A corporate authority is necessary for these tasks. Territorial spirits are fallen angels—principalities, powers, dominions, thrones, authorities and rulers—that exercise influence over cities, regions, even nations (see Eph. 1:21; 6:12; Col. 2:15). These demonic spirits influence various aspects of culture in much the same way that certain types of soil determine which crops can be grown in particular regions.

I enjoy visiting various parts of the world and seeing the varieties of flowers, shrubs and trees. Canada has such beautiful flowers, which bloom profusely. When I have inquired about specific flowers in that region, I have discovered that they do not grow in warm climates. The soil and prevailing weather of Texas do not nurture the growth of certain Canadian plants, and vice versa. We find the same thing is true when it comes to characteristics of geographical areas. Some places are more prone to crime, poverty or even the preaching of the Word than other areas. The reason for this is not the people who live there; these conditions exist due to the spiritual climate of that area. Changing any spiritual climate and causing it to be in agreement with the Kingdom is a challenge for all believers.

> *For change to be manifest on Earth, corporate authority on a spiritual level is required.*

Today the Lord is gathering intercessors and leaders together to pray and see cities and territories change. When believers get together in corporate unity, a power is released that brings a manifestation of God's will to Earth. Cindy Jacobs wrote about corporate authority that changed the spiritual climate in a city:

Dee Jepsen felt that the Lord was directing her to establish a 24-hour "prayer and praise tent" on the mall in Washington, D.C., for a period after the 1988 Washington for Jesus rally. During this praise and worship were continually lifted up to God on behalf of the nation and the capital city. One of the most measurable results was that there were no murders during those seven days in a city dubbed the murder capital of the world! The Lord promised that He would heal our land if we pray.[4]

After September 11, 2001, President George W. Bush built a coalition of leaders from many nations. He understood the importance of corporate authority. The problem of terrorism is being solved by a coalition of leaders and governments. The international community is the corporate authority that is needed to deal with practical aspects of winning this new type of war. Likewise, the corporate Body of Christ is necessary to take down the spiritual powers around terrorism. Dealing with certain powers requires more than an individual nation, military might or governmental authority. For change to be manifest on Earth, corporate authority on a spiritual level is required.

NEW TESTAMENT LEADERSHIP

Individuals are frequently seen leading God's people in the Old Testament. The Lord used men and women such as Moses, Joshua, David and Deborah in powerful ways. However, we see a mantle shift in the New Testament. Jesus implemented a corporate-authority standard when He established leadership for the New Testament Church:

> And He gave some as apostles, and some as prophets, and some as evangelists, and some as pastors and teachers, for the equipping of the saints for the work of service, to the building up of the body of Christ; until we all attain to the unity of the faith, and of the knowledge of the Son of God, to a mature man, to the measure of the stature which belongs to the fullness of Christ (Eph. 4:11-13).

Jesus desired a corporate leadership team to lead His people. There is always a senior leader on a team, yet the team is to function as a corporate entity. A principle of this change is found in Hebrews:

Then He said, "Behold, I have come to do Your will." He takes away the first in order to establish the second (Heb. 10:9).

When Jesus came to Earth, He lived here as a man. He was tested and overcame evil as a human being. After His death, burial and resurrection, He went to heaven. Jesus lived on Earth as a physical man. The physical man was taken away, so He could establish another man—a spiritual man. The spiritual man is the Corporate Man—the Body of Christ. None of us as individuals can fully represent the Lord Jesus. To express all of His authority will take all of us together.

ROOTS OF LAWLESSNESS

I was raised in Mobile, Alabama, and still have deep roots there. Some time ago Pastor David Richey invited me to visit and help release a spiritual breakthrough over the city.

We sought the Lord for months about the timing. Earlier in the year, I had sensed the Lord revealing an appointed time. So we made plans, and in October 2002, I went to Mobile to speak. This coincided with a time of fear and apprehension in our nation as snipers went about killing and wounding innocent individuals in Washington, D.C., Maryland and Virginia.

During the Saturday-night meeting in Mobile, we entered into a time of corporate intercession. I began to declare to the evil principalities and powers that we, the Body of Christ, are the corporate voice of the Lord in the earthly realm. As the voice of the Lord on Earth, I declared, "We arrest the sniper in the authority of the Lord. We command the murdering spirit in the Washington area to stop!" Within a matter of days, the accused snipers were arrested. One of the interesting details surrounding their arrest was the uncovering of key information from an earlier murder in Alabama.

We were not the only intercessors praying about this horri-
fying situation, of course. Many prayer groups around the
nation were praying corporately. One group included my friend
Chuck Pierce. He sent out an alert for 17 days of prayer. He said
if we would pray for 17 days and declare victory, the sniper
would be found. A few days after the 17 days of prayer ended, he
was speaking at a meeting in Ann Arbor, Michigan. His newslet-
ter gives the following report:

> We are so thankful that the one who was being used by
> the enemy to kill and rob life and bring terror in that area
> was found at the end of the 17-day period. This shows us
> that God is doing something in His people by bringing
> us into a new place of *corporate prayer*. Some battles will
> only be won through our uniting in corporate prayer in
> this nation. The power of unity releases an anointing,
> and the anointing breaks the yoke. We have grief over the
> loss of human life that has occurred through this act, but
> rejoice that God has stopped the hand of the enemy.
>
> Tuesday night and Wednesday, we met . . . in Ann
> Arbor at Apostle Barbara Yoder's church. God led us to
> do prophetic acts surrounding this lawless spirit. Jim
> Chosa, our Regional Coordinator for the High Plains
> region, declared a root of violence had never been dealt
> with. Being a Native American leader, he felt he had the
> authority to decree that the very root linked with this
> lawless act would be pulled up. Cindy Jacobs led us in a
> tremendous prayer in this area. And Peter Wagner stood
> and made the following apostolic declaration. "I declare
> that this lawless spirit will no longer be able to operate. I
> declare it to stop and be found." . . . We are in an incredi-
> ble time of change. The Church is rising to a new level

across the land. Your prayers are causing heaven and earth to meet, and the will of God to be performed [emphasis added].[5]

At about the same time the sniper suspects were arrested at a Maryland rest stop, federal authorities removed a tree stump from the yard of a Tacoma, Washington, house. The suspects had once lived at that address and reportedly used the tree for target practice, and an examination was made in an attempt to secure bullet fragments that might connect the suspects to the D.C.-area shootings.

BREAKTHROUGH

Whether it is in Mobile, Alabama, or your city, whether it involves a national scare or a more subtle threat, breakthrough happens when God's people come together corporately. From the beginning the Lord knew that it was not good for man to be alone. For each person to fulfill God's plan for transformation on Earth, a corporate authority is needed. Together, we will see God's will on Earth executed through a corporate authority that is more powerful than the power of the enemy!

Ask the Lord to connect you with those who have a heart to see your territory transformed by the power of God.

Heavenly Father, thank You for not leaving us alone. I thank You for Your plan to see the Body of Christ come together. My desire is to be part of something bigger than myself. I am asking You to connect me with those who have the same heart. Put me with those who desire to see our region changed by Your power. Help me to add my part in intercession to the part others have.

Together may we release the power of Your Spirit that will overcome the power of the enemy. Teach us how to flow together as a symphony and not be in discord. May You be glorified through a corporate people who fully express Your authority on Earth. In Jesus' name I pray. Amen.

Notes

1. C. Peter Wagner, *Apostles and Prophets* (Ventura, CA: Regal Books, 2000), pp. 88-89.
2. *Webster's New World College Dictionary,* 4th ed., s.v. "corporate."
3. Judson Cornwall, *Let Us Get Together* (Old Tappan, NJ: Fleming H. Revell Company, 1983), p. 66.
4. Cindy Jacobs, *Possessing the Gates of the Enemy* (Tarrytown, NY: Chosen Books, 1991), pp. 193-194.
5. Chuck Pierce, "Ten Days of Praise to Secure the Testimony of Victory," *Glory of Zion* (October 25, 2002), p. 1.

CHAPTER 9

TERRITORIAL
AUTHORITY

Excitedly the three of us rode down the highway, anticipating a shopping spree in Carmel, California. We were friends and, like many such women, had set the day aside to have fun together. Laughter and much talking filled the car—until a flashing light appeared in the rearview mirror! A county highway patrolman was behind us. My friend pulled her car off to the side of the road. We were still puzzled as the officer approached the car.

"Lady, do you know what the speed limit is here?" he asked my friend who was driving.

"No, officer, I don't know," she answered.

"Do you know how fast you were driving?" he asked.

"No, I don't," she again replied.

Then the policeman explained that he had been following her for several miles. He had even pulled his car in front of hers to see if she would slow down. Each time, she passed his car. Finally, he realized she was not going to decrease her speed. That is when he pulled us over.

My friend explained our shopping plans. Two of us lived in another state. We were so happy to be together that we were laughing and talking. She failed to check the speed limit for that territory and had not been watching the speedometer in the car.

After checking my friend's driver's license and finding out where we were going, the officer gave her a warning. "The speed limit in my territory is 65 miles per hour," he stated. "Do not drive over that limit. When you get out of my territory, you can drive any limit you want to. You probably will anyway. Just be sure you drive within the limit while you're in my territory."

After he had gone, we sat there for a few minutes, remembering his last words to us: "By the way, lady, don't ever pass a highway patrol car."

Soon we were laughing as we recounted what the patrolman had said. He really did not care what we did once we left his jurisdiction. He had no authority in other areas. However, he had the authority to enforce the law within his territory. The policeman understood territorial authority.

A LARGER SPHERE

Territorial authority affects a much larger sphere than does the rule we exercise in our own lives. Usually a corporate authority is needed to impact a region, or territory, in a significant way. The policeman who stopped our car had territorial authority. He had authority to enforce the speed of traffic within his assigned parameters. The corporate traffic department of his county delegated this power to him and his colleagues.

In the same way, God promised that a strong, vibrant Church that operates in righteousness has the ability through intercession to heal the entire land:

> And [if] My people who are called by My name humble themselves and pray and seek My face and turn from their wicked ways, then I will hear from heaven, will forgive their sin and will heal their land (2 Chron. 7:14).

One person or one church can bring a measure of healing. However, for the land to be healed, many believers in an area must unite in repentance and intercession. Their lives should be lived in righteousness for healing to come to the land.

AUTHORITY OVER EVIL

Throughout the Bible, we find examples of God's people operating in territorial authority. One instance of this is when the Israelites were journeying through the wilderness. They encountered warfare with the Canaanites and exercised territorial authority to win a great victory:

> When the Canaanite, the king of Arad, who lived in the Negev, heard that Israel was coming by the way of Atharim, then he fought against Israel and took some of them captive. So Israel made a vow to the LORD and said, "If You will indeed deliver this people into my hand, then I will utterly destroy their cities." The LORD heard the voice of Israel and delivered up the Canaanites; then they utterly destroyed them and their cities. Thus the name of the place was called Hormah (Num. 21:1-3).

When God's people live righteous lives before Him, the Lord intervenes and gives them authority over the evil in their land:

> Hear, O Israel! You are crossing over the Jordan today to go in to dispossess nations greater and mightier than you, great cities fortified to heaven, a people great and tall, the sons of the Anakim, whom you know and of whom you have heard it said, "Who can stand before the sons of Anak?" Know therefore today that it is the LORD your God who is crossing over before you as a consuming fire. He will destroy them and He will subdue them before you, so that you may drive them out and destroy them quickly, just as the LORD has spoken to you (Deut. 9:1-3).

HEALING OF CITIES

Cities and nations are very important to God. Regardless of the evil found in these areas, each has a destiny in God. When evil is in a city or region, the Lord can bring healing through repentance and intercession. Often we find places in the Bible where the Lord calls an entire territory to repent.

Jesus spoke to cities and called them to repent:

Cities and nations are very important to God.

> Then He began to denounce the cities in which most of His miracles were done, because they did not repent. "Woe to you, Chorazin! Woe to you, Bethsaida! For if the miracles had occurred in Tyre and Sidon which occurred in you, they would have repented long ago in sackcloth and ashes. Nevertheless I say to you, it will be

more tolerable for Tyre and Sidon in the day of judgment than for you. And you, Capernaum, will not be exalted to heaven, will you? You will descend to Hades; for if the miracles had occurred in Sodom which occurred in you, it would have remained to this day. Nevertheless I say to you that it will be more tolerable for the land of Sodom in the day of judgment, than for you" (Matt. 11:20-24).

Evil spirits find entrance into cities and regions in the same way they find entrance into individual lives. Demonic spirits enter territories through past sins and current sins or through generational curses and iniquities. They enter through practices of idolatry, witchcraft, victimization and trauma. Demonization of a territory results in suffering poverty, broken relationships, sickness, disease and other maladies.

CORRUPTION OF CULTURE

Even the culture in an area can be corrupted. George Otis Jr. has researched cultures throughout the world. He discovered that strongholds in culture are often able to hold people in the grip of evil through each succeeding generation. One of the ways this is accomplished is through participation in cultural festivals. He stressed the impact of demonic spirits in a territory when people of the area give their minds and will over to these spirits:

There is little doubt that such surrender, especially when expressed corporately, often leads to the release of significant spiritual power. Nearly all of the national believers and missionaries I have interviewed associate religious festivals with a heightened sense of oppression, increased persecution and manifestations of demonic signs and wonders. One believer living in the holy city of Mecca requested special prayer covering for the upcoming *hajj.* "At that time of the pilgrimage," he explained, "it is as if devils are walking through the streets." . . .

Religious festivals, ceremonies and pilgrimages are not the benign cultural spectacles they are made out to be. There is nothing innocent or "natural" about them. When the colorful veneer is stripped away, they are conscious transactions with the spirit world, occasions for successive generations to reaffirm choices and pacts made by their ancestors. In this sense festivals are a kind of generational passing of the baton, a chance to dust off ancient welcome mats and extend the devil's right to rule over specific peoples and places. Their significance should not be underestimated.[1]

The enemy has a plan to destroy the Christian witness of the Church in every aspect of a culture in cities and regions. Attempts are made to get any trace of Christian witness removed from public documents and buildings and from governmental and educational systems. The enemy also tries to remove Christian facts from history books in order to distort the true historical perspective. The resulting lack of Christian witness in such areas leaves a void that the enemy quickly seeks to fill.

> *The enemy has a plan to destroy the Christian witness in every aspect of a culture.*

A PLAN FOR TERRITORIES

After the fall of communism I took teams into Russia. We went into villages to preach the good news and establish churches.

Access to the Bible had officially been denied these people for 70 years. Two generations had heard very little or nothing at all about the wonderful transforming power of the Lord. Due to the longstanding spiritual famine, people were spiritually hungry and open. Cults also streamed into Russia during this time. Islam and other religions grew. Although Russia had a history of Christianity, the Christian witness had been officially suppressed under communism. The enemy used this situation to exercise demonic authority over the territory.

Even though the enemy has a plan, God also has a plan for territories. His plan is to be executed through the territorial authority of the believers in any specific region. This is to come through intercession and restoration, not via physical force:

> Those from among you will rebuild the ancient ruins;
> you will raise up the age-old foundations; and you will
> be called the repairer of the breach, the restorer of the
> streets in which to dwell (Isa. 58:12).

Through intercession believers have the authority of the Lord to bring peace into riot-infested streets. They can bring healing into communities filled with drugs and immorality. The Lordship of Jesus can be established in areas where people worship demonic deities.

The videocassette series *Transformation* by George Otis Jr. documents the transforming power of the Lord in cities around the world. Poverty, ignorance, sickness, fear and false worship captured these cities. As believers gathered together and prayed, change came to the territories. The believers understood their authority as the Lord's representatives, and they stood against principalities and powers that were operating in the heavenly realm over these areas. The unity of believers in strategic intercession helped dismantle old demonic rulers that had controlled the people of those areas for years.

Evidence of transformation came in Almolonga, Guatemala, as the economy changed. Produce became abundant, and the sale of the produce increased the income of the community. Instead of one harvest per year, many of the crops now yield three harvests each year. The city even closed its jails because no crimes were being committed!

Extending to Nations

The Moravians were a group of people who experienced territorial authority that extended into many nations of the world. The Moravian refugees were believers who came out of the 100-year religious war in Europe. They wandered into eastern Germany and met a man named Count Nikolaus von Zinzendorf, who invited them to settle on the land around his estate. They built a village called Herrnhut, which means "the Lord's watch." In 1727 one of the Moravian prophets prophesied, "The Lord will place a light on this hill which will illumine the whole land."

Later that year, on August 13, 1727, the community gathered for worship in a Lutheran church in a nearby city. Zinzendorf got up to speak but was unable to finish his message because the "fire of God" fell. The presence of God exploded into the building with great signs and wonders. In *The Lost Art of Intercession*, Jim Goll recorded the story of Zinzendorf and these powerful intercessors:

> I learned that God gave them "three strands" around which they wove their lives, and these strands helped the Moravians become world-changers:
> 1. They had relational unity, spiritual community and sacrificial living.
> 2 The power of their persistent prayer produced a

divine passion and zeal for missionary outreach to the lost. Many of them even sold themselves into slavery in places like Surinam in South America just so they could carry the light of the gospel into closed societies. The Moravians were the first missionaries to the slaves of St. Thomas in the Virgin Islands; they went to strange places called Lapland and Greenland and to many places in Africa.

3. The third strand was described by a motto that they lived by: "No one works unless someone prays." This took the form of corporate commitment to sustained prayer and ministry to the Lord. The prayer went on unbroken for 24 hours a day, seven days a week, every day of each year for over 100 years![2]

The Moravians wanted more than just the presence of God for the moment. They wanted to know how to sustain it. They also wanted God's presence to extend throughout their territory and into the nations of the world. After searching the Bible, the Moravians did something that had not been done in the Church for centuries: They started a prayer meeting that was held 24 hours a day and continued it for more than 100 years.

Although there were only a few dozen of them, their efforts affected the entire world. Missionaries were sent to many nations of the world. One of the first places they went was England. The Moravian missionaries were instrumental in leading John Wesley to the Lord. After his conversion, Wesley visited Herrnhut to receive an empowering. He took the revival fire back to England, and that nation was transformed. Secular historians say England was spared a bloody revolution similar to the French Revolution because revival was brought to their land.

The Moravians also sent missionaries to Greenland, North

America, South America, Tibet and Africa. The revival, known as the First Great Awakening, eventually made its way from England to America through George Whitfield. Church attendance in this country doubled and then tripled within a few years. Benjamin Franklin said that America changed from being thoughtless and indifferent about religion to the point that it seemed to him as if the entire world were growing religious. One could not walk through a street in an evening without hearing various families singing spiritual songs.

The revival changed America. Some of the men whose lives had been transformed by that revival helped write the Constitution of the United States. All along, the continual prayer back in Herrnhut was releasing spiritual authority to heal and transform lands throughout the world.

CHANGES FROM THE HOLY SPIRIT

When the Lord connects believers in a city or a region as He did in Herrnhut, an exponential power is released to change the spiritual climate of the area. The power of the Holy Spirit is required to effectively penetrate the territory. Government programs such as welfare assistance do not change the spiritual climate. These measures can alleviate some symptoms of the problems. However, only the power of the Holy Spirit can bring about significant change. God changes hearts and minds. A shift in old mind-sets must happen before a community or nation can be dramatically improved. The old mind-sets hold people captive, imprisoning and separating them

The power of the Holy Spirit is required to effectively penetrate a territory.

from the blessings of the Lord. Only present truth found in God's Word and His power are able to destroy the old oppositional mentalities:

> For though we walk in the flesh, we do not war according to the flesh, for the weapons of our warfare are not of the flesh, but divinely powerful for the destruction of fortresses. We are destroying speculations and every lofty thing raised up against the knowledge of God, and we are taking every thought captive to the obedience of Christ (2 Cor. 10:3-5).

If transformation is to come to cities and nations, intercession and spiritual warfare must be involved. The minds of people are blinded, so they cannot see the truth. They are cut off from the powerful presence of the Lord:

> And even if our gospel is veiled, it is veiled to those who are perishing, in whose case the god of this world has blinded the minds of the unbelieving so that they might not see the light of the gospel of the glory of Christ, who is the image of God (2 Cor. 4:3-4).

Authority in intercession has the power to break the blinders and destroy the strategies of the enemy that hold people captive in a region. In Acts 12:19 we read the story of enemy strategies to destroy the plan of God—strategies that continued for several generations. Three generations of Herods sought to kill and destroy God's people. During the reign of the third Herod, the believers gathered together to pray. The prayers of the saints released a territorial authority that brought change to the city.

FERVENT PRAYER

So Peter was kept in the prison, but prayer for him was being made fervently by the church to God (Acts 12:5).

According to Spiros Zodhiates, the word "fervently" is from the Greek word *ektenes*, which means "stretched out, continual, intense." It is derived from the verb *ektenio*, meaning to "stretch out, extend, as the hand; to cast out, let down, as an anchor from a ship."[3]

The prayers for Peter stretched out over a period of time. They stretched out from the house where believers were praying toward the prison that held Peter captive. The prayers were continual and intense. Not everyone was praying, yet the Lord heard and answered the prayers of a group representing the Church. As one voice, they cried out to the Lord. Positioning themselves in prayer, they were like an anchor let down from a boat. They refused to move from the corporate position of prayer until the answer came.

As a result of this type of prayer, the territory was changed. Not only was Peter set free from the prison, but also the territory was set free from the demonic governmental ruler. It was only a matter of time until Herod died. His death removed the evil influence in the territory and allowed the Church to grow by multiplying the number of new believers:

> And immediately an angel of the Lord struck him because he did not give God the glory, and he was eaten by worms and died. But the word of the Lord continued to grow and to be multiplied (Acts 12:23-24).

The Lord will heal cities, territories and nations as His people gather together in intercession and spiritual warfare, and an authority that brings the manifestation of God's will to Earth is released into the atmosphere. Pray fervently that the will of the Lord will be manifest in your city.

Heavenly Father, thank You for the privilege of being used by You to bring change to my city. I repent of participating in any cultural event where I have entered into pacts or agreements with evil spirits in the name of culture. Forgive me for my sin. I confess that Jesus is my Lord. I will not worship or give allegiance to any other god. I break the power of those vows by the authority of the blood of Jesus. I cancel their effect and call them null and void.

Lord, cleanse me of all my sin and renew my spirit. Grant me the grace, Lord, to anchor in prayer. I desire to stretch my prayers across my territory until I see the manifestation of Your will on Earth.

Thank You for the authority You have given me to participate in bringing transformation to cities and nations. May Your will be done on Earth, even as it is done in heaven. In the wonderful name of Jesus, I pray. Amen.

Notes

1. George Otis Jr., *The Twilight Labyrinth* (Grand Rapids, MI: Chosen Books, 1997), pp. 202-203.
2. Jim W. Goll, *The Lost Art of Intercession* (Shippensburg, PA: Revival Press, 1997), pp. 2-3.
3. Spiros Zodhiates, *Hebrew-Greek Keyword Study Bible (New American Standard Version)* (Chattanooga, TN: AMG Publishers, 1990), p. 1830.

THE RIGHT TIME AND THE RIGHT SEASON

After I had spoken at several meetings in Germany several years ago, my friends convinced me to take a few days off. We drove down to Switzerland to see the beautiful mountains and waterfalls. While there, we rode a cog train to the top of one the majestic Swiss Alps.

Shortly after we arrived at the top of the mountain, I noticed a couple standing next to the guardrail. They sipped apple juice and kept looking out at the other mountains in the distance. Periodically they would extend their arms over the rail and feel the wind. They did not appear to be in a hurry; they simply stood there and kept checking the wind.

After a while the couple mounted hang gliders and took off into the distance. I watched, amazed! It was impossible to see the ground from the height where we stood. The peaks of the other mountains seemed so sharp and looming. And hang gliders have no engines! As they soared gracefully on the air currents, I voiced my concerns:

- "Why had they waited so long to take off?"
- "What would happen if they lost control of the hang gliders?"
- "How were they able to maneuver around the mountains without hitting them or colliding with each other?"

One of my friends answered my questions. The couple had been waiting for the wind to be just right. They had been checking the ridge lift and thermals for sustaining air. The crucial times when the wind velocity becomes particularly important are during launching and landing and as the air hits anything that disrupts its flow. Because the force of the wind is proportional to the square of its velocity, higher wind speeds need to be treated with a great deal of respect. Hang-glider pilots fly using their senses—not instruments—and each one takes a different amount of time to develop the use and coordination of those senses to become a safe, good pilot. When all the requirements of the preflight check were met, the couple in the Alps used their trained senses and, in this way, assured a safe takeoff and the accomplishment of their intended goals for the flight.

THE WIND OF THE SPIRIT

Through the years, I have often thought of that day on the top of those beautiful Alps. The experience reminds me that there are times in intercession when we must discern the wind of God's Holy Spirit. It is important to know when His wind is just right so that we can see our prayers reach their intended goal.

Jesus rebuked His followers because they understood natural weather forecasts but were not able to discern spiritual weather:

> But He replied to them, "When it is evening, you say, 'It will be fair weather, for the sky is red.' And in the morning, 'There will be a storm today, for the sky is red and threatening.' Do you know how to discern the appearance of the sky, but cannot discern the signs of the times?" (Matt. 16:2-3).

Intercessors need a correct understanding of spiritual times and a discerning of the spiritual season to determine what is right at the moment.

UNDERSTANDING THE TIMES

David's men had that kind of understanding:

> Of the sons of Issachar, men who understood the times (1 Chron. 12:32).

These men did not only understand the current time on a clock or the days listed on a calendar, but they also understood the strategic, opportune times when the Lord wanted to release His will on Earth. God alerts His people to pray during these strategic times. *Eth* is the Hebrew word for this usage of the word "time." The corresponding Greek word is *kairos*. I wrote about the use of these words in my book *Prophetic Intercession*:

> The word *eth* in Hebrew is the same word as *kairos* in the Greek. Ecclesiastes tells us that there is an *eth* time for

every occurrence in the earth. *Eth* means God has orches-
trated a strategic time for prayers to break through. By
the power of the Holy Spirit, He will alert intercessors to
pray during those times. Praying the right kind of prayer
at the right time is vital. Since every believer can hear the
voice of the Lord, every believer can pray by the moving
of the Holy Spirit.

Powerful things happen when we participate with
the Lord at these specific times. God has put the Church
on the earth to finish the work of putting Satan under
His feet.[1]

Intercessors need not only to understand the current strategic time, but they also need to realize they have the power to
change current, natural time. Through the discerning of the present strategic time and praying with the spiritual authority given
them, intercessors can bring about the release of a new spiritual
time and season.

Changing the time can sometimes be challenging. I remember my grandmother never liked daylight saving time. After the
clocks had been turned, she would ask, "What time is it? I don't
want to know the *new time*. I want to know the *real time*." To her,
new time was daylight saving time. Real time was what she was
accustomed to in the past.

Changing the Time of Death
Believers often feel that they are locked in to the times in which
they live. They never realize that the Lord has given them a
power to bring about change on Earth. King Hezekiah prayed
and saw the Lord change time for him (see 2 Kings 20:1-11).
Hezekiah had become ill and was destined to die. The prophet
Isaiah prophesied that indeed he would die. However, Hezekiah
did not merely settle for things the way they were. He prayed and

reminded the Lord that he had been faithful to serve Him. As a result, Isaiah returned to deliver the promise of the Lord to Hezekiah: God would heal him and give him 15 more years to live. After asking for a sign from the Lord concerning his healing, Hezekiah was given a choice by God: The Lord would turn the sundial back 10 steps or move it forward 10 steps:

> So Hezekiah answered, "It is easy for the shadow to decline ten steps; no, but let the shadow turn backward ten steps." Isaiah the prophet cried to the LORD, and He brought the shadow on the stairway back ten steps by which it had gone down on the stairway of Ahaz (2 Kings 20:10-11).

Although Hezekiah was supposed to die, he was able to change the time of his death and make it 15 years later!

DEFEATING THE ENEMY

Another person in the Bible who brought change in time was Joshua. Joshua and his men went to help the men of Gibeon fight a battle (see Josh. 10:1-15). The Lord helped Joshua and the men to experience victory. Later Joshua spoke a powerful command to the sun to stand still. He needed more time to avenge the enemies of God:

> Then Joshua spoke to the LORD in the day when the LORD delivered up the Amorites before the sons of Israel, and he said in the sight of Israel, "O sun, stand still at Gibeon, and O moon in the valley of Aijalon." So the sun stood still, and the moon stopped, until the nation avenged themselves of their enemies. Is it not written in the book of Jashar? And the sun stopped in

the middle of the sky and did not hasten to go down for about a whole day (Josh. 10:12-13).

Joshua changed natural time to God's strategic time.

Wanting God's will, many believers look at situations and say, "I'm just waiting until God is ready." Frequently He *is* ready; He is just waiting for us to arise and move in the power of the Holy Spirit. Many times we ask the Lord to do what He has given us the authority to do. Joshua knew the will of the Lord to defeat His enemies. Joshua spoke with authority to the situation and saw the Lord's victory.

> *Sometimes the Lord is more interested in changing us than changing the situation.*

Why did Joshua wait until that day to command the sun to stand still? He obviously knew when the time was right. A time of waiting preceeded the time of release. Times of waiting can be difficult. It can seem like the time is wasted. Yet the time before the release of God's will is not squandered time. Rather, waiting should be with purpose.

WAITING WITH PURPOSE

In the Old Testament, Esther was required to wait for 12 months before approaching the king (see Esther 2:12). During this time of waiting, she went through a period of purification. It seems that waiting always brings out our impurities. Impatience, frustration and deferred hope can surface during those waiting times. It helps to remember that things are not as final as they may seem at any given moment. Finances can shift. Bodies can be healed. Relationships can turn. Sometimes the Lord is more interested in changing us than changing the situation. It is always a good idea to ask the Lord to reveal any areas of our lives that may need to be purified while waiting.

Waiting also helps to develop our discernment. Esther understood that her future role would depend on her ability to know the desires of the king. Therefore, she did not do what other women did, which was take whatever they wanted with them when they appeared before the king (see Esther 2:13). Esther discerned that the king's eunuch knew more about what to take than she did. She received his advice and took with her only those things he recommended (see Esther 2:15). Discernment is vital in defeating the enemy in the days ahead.

Mistakes from the past do not signify failure. These mistakes are only lessons from the school of the Holy Spirit. They make us wiser and smarter than we were before, which means that we did not fail in those situations. God uses tough times to develop discernment in us so that we do not repeat the same courses. As a result, we get promoted.

Esther later understood that it was a strategic time for her to move into a new level of authority. She could not be just a nice queen. She had been positioned by God to bring His will to Earth. When she learned of the plot to destroy her people, she knew she could not remain quiet. She had to lift her voice and use her place of authority to save her people. Mordecai, Esther's cousin, reminded her of the authority vested in her:

> For if you remain silent at this time, relief and deliverance will arise for the Jews from another place and you and your father's house will perish. And who knows whether you have not attained royalty for such a time as this? (Esther 4:14).

In intercession we cannot be silent. We exercise the authority given us by King Jesus and lift our voices to bring change to a situation. When we exercise this privilege in intercession, it must always be in the spirit of humility. We cannot love our own lives to the death. Whatever the Lord asks, we must be willing to do. Esther acted in the spirit of humility. She was willing to accept her assignment without concern for self:

> Go, assemble all the Jews who are found in Susa, and fast for me; do not eat or drink for three days, night or day. I and my maidens also will fast in the same way. And thus I will go in to the king, which is not according to the law; and if I perish, I perish (Esther 4:16).

Concern for others more than for herself caused Esther to take a risk. She clothed herself with new garments for the new strategic season. No longer was she dressed as an orphan. She was no longer who she had been in the past. A new day had dawned. Esther was entering the time for which she had been born, fulfilling the purpose for which she had been waiting.

THIRD-DAY PEOPLE

You and I have lived all our lives for the moment we are in right now. We need to remove any old clothing of shame, rejection or abandonment, and allow the Lord to bury the rags of yesterday. We are standing as a Third-Day people who have risen, clothed with authority, to do exploits for the kingdom of God (see Dan. 11:32, *KJV*).

The Bible tells us that 1,000 years are like a day to the Lord (see Ps. 90:4; 2 Pet. 3:8). That means, since Jesus' birth, humankind has completed two days (two millennia) and have now entered the Third Day (third millennium). The number three speaks of resurrection. Now is a time for resurrection power to be released in the people of God:

Come, let us return to the LORD. For He has torn us, but
He will heal us; He has wounded us, but He will bandage
us. He will revive us after two days; He will raise us up on
the third day, that we may live before Him (Hos. 6:1-2).

I like what Chuck Pierce and Rebecca Wagner Sytsema write
about the Third-Day Church in their book *The Future War of the
Church*.

As the Church transitions from the "second day" to the
"third day," we can expect to see not only revival but also
Resurrection power that will overthrow the demonic
forces that have kept us from seeing God's will done on
Earth. The new wineskin to receive this power is now
being formed by the Holy Spirit, even as He is preparing
the wine to be poured in. God is transforming the
Church, preparing us to receive revelation for future victory. The Church is arising and the Kingdom is coming.
   To arise means to get up from a prostrate position,
come up out of oppression, to awaken or ascend. The
Church is arising with favor and strength for a latter-day
advancement against the wicked forces that are holding
the harvest captive. We must begin to see ourselves as the
Third-Day Church, emerging with the power to fulfill
the mandate of the Great Commission.[2]

Queen Esther rose from her lowly position in the past to a
new position of favor and authority.

Now it came about on the third day that Esther put on
her royal robes and stood in the inner court of the king's
palace in front of the king's rooms, and the king was sit-
ting on his royal throne in the throne room, opposite

the entrance to the palace. When the king saw Esther the queen standing in the court, she obtained favor in his sight; and the king extended to Esther the golden scepter which was in his hand. So Esther came near and touched the top of the scepter (Esther 5:1-2).

Esther received favor from the king, as well as the authority to carry out her assignment from God. Intercessors receive authoritative power to govern, or rule, in situations to advance God's purpose on Earth.

A NOW GOD FOR A NOW SEASON

The Lord raises up intercessors who understand current times and seasons. They have a revelation that He is a *now* God for a *now* season. This Third-Day level of intercession also has a *now* time frame when the will of God can be released on Earth.

Too many times we have only a revelation of the God of the past. By this, I do not mean God changes; rather, we keep retelling testimonies of miracles the Lord performed 10, 20 or more years ago. They are exciting, and we do not want to forget them, but they are not *now*. When the children of Israel crossed the Jordan River, they erected a memorial of 12 stones to remind them of God's faithfulness in bringing them across the Jordan and into the Promised Land:

> *It is important to keep a thankful heart for God's faithfulness in the past.*

Then you shall say to them, "Because the waters of the Jordan were cut off before the ark of the covenant of the LORD; when it crossed the Jordan, the waters of the Jordan were cut off." So these stones shall become a memorial to the sons of Israel forever (Josh. 4:7).

It is obvious from the Scriptures that it is important to keep a thankful heart for God's faithfulness in the past. Still, we don't want to focus so exclusively on the things God did in the past that we fail to anticipate what He will do in the future. If we do that, we will find ourselves making statements like the following:

• Someday the Lord is going to answer my prayer.
• I know the Lord will perform a miracle one day.
• How wonderful it will be when the Lord's will is done.
• Someday revival is going to happen.

We need to be filled with expectancy that the Lord will *always* be faithful, and He will fulfill His promises. While the news media paints a dark picture of the future, the Church is heading into her finest hour! God is going to cause His glory to fill the earth, even as the waters cover the sea (see Hab. 2:14).

Still, in intercession we need a revelation that the Lord is not just the God of the past, nor is He simply the God of the future. He is also the God of the *now*. When Moses was sent to Egypt to deliver God's people, he asked the Lord a question: "They may say to me, 'What is His name?' What shall I say to them?" (Exod. 3:13). In response the Lord reminded Moses that He is God of the *now*:

> God said to Moses, "I AM WHO I AM"; and He said, "Thus you shall say to the sons of Israel, 'I AM has sent me to you'" (Exod. 3:14).

Intercession has a *now* time to cause the will of God to be released on Earth. Understanding that the Lord is the same yesterday, today and forever causes faith to arise that He is powerful today. Many churches teach that the Lord did miracles in the past. Some even acknowledge that He will fulfill certain promises in the future. Yet they teach that God does not perform miracles today. I am not sure what they do with Hebrews 13:8: "Jesus Christ is the same yesterday and *today* and forever" (emphasis added).

When the king asked Esther what she wanted, he was not asking her what he had done for her in the past, nor was he promising to do something for her in the distant future. He merely wanted to know what she wanted at the moment:

> Then the king said to her, "What is troubling you, Queen Esther? And what is your request? Even to half of the kingdom it shall be given to you" (Esther 5:3).

The king was ready to give Esther a *now* answer to her request.

FROM TERROR TO PEACE

There are times in intercession when we will know what to ask, what to do and how to decree the will of the Lord. God will give a prophetic knowing of the right season to discern when He is ready to move in the earth. On October 29, 2002, I received an e-mail with a message forwarded to me from the Presidential Prayer Team. The message told the story of a group of truckers who prayed for the arrest of the sniper who had been terrorizing communities and stopping normal life for several weeks:

> Fifty Christian truckers got together to pray that somehow the sniper terrorizing the Washington, D.C., area would be caught. Ron Lantz would be retiring in a few days and didn't even live in the area, but he felt sure that God would answer their prayers. In fact, he told the others there that

God was going to use him to catch the sniper.

A few days later he was listening to the radio as he was driving again through the region and felt compelled to pull off the highway to a rest stop. It was just a couple of miles from where the prayer meeting had taken place. As he pulled in, he was shocked to see a car similar to what was being described on the radio right there before his eyes.

Carefully trying to read the license plate, a chill went up his back as the numbers matched. He quickly called 911 and remained there for what he said was the longest 15 minutes of his life until the police arrived. He even pulled his truck across the exit; there would now be no escape for these elusive murderers. The rest is now history—the snipers were taken into custody without incident.

Ron's testimony is being beamed around the world today. It shows the power of prayer. And in a class act, showing his true character, when asked what he would do with the award money, he said the half million dollars would simply be given to the victim's families.

The snipers killed 10 and wounded 3 around our nation's capital over the past three weeks, leaving the entire region in a state of terror. Yet out of the great darkness has also come a great beam of light as the world has heard a clear testimony of the power of prayer.[3]

Ron and his fellow truckers sensed it was a time when the Lord was ready to answer prayer. They asked a specific request of the Lord. They wanted the arrest of the sniper. Ron knew what to do when he moved his truck to block the exit. The Lord answered the prayers of these faithful truck drivers and the prayers of others asking the same specific request. The season of terror was changed to a season of peace in that region.

The next day newspapers reported people out on the streets

once again. Business had resumed. School children had returned to their classes. The enemy had been stopped through the power of intercession. The plans of the enemy came to death. In a similar way Queen Esther also received the authority of the king to bring death to the enemy:

> So King Ahasuerus said to Queen Esther and to Mordecai the Jew, "Behold, I have given the house of Haman to Esther, and him they have hanged on the gallows because he had stretched out his hands against the Jews" (Esther 8:7).

In response to intercession, our God, who is I AM, releases the future into the present situation. Ask the Lord to extend His scepter of authority to you. Believe Him to answer your prayer and cause the future to manifest itself in your present situation.

> *Heavenly Father, I ask You to cause my spirit to be sensitive to Your timing. Give me an Issachar anointing to know the right time when You want to bring change in the earth. Thank You that I am part of Your Third-Day Church. I lay aside old garments of fear, discouragement and abandonment. I receive the new garments of favor, humility and authority. You truly are I AM. Thank You for empowering me to know what to ask when I pray. Give me discernment to know what to do and the faith to decree Your will. I receive Your authority to pray and bring the future into my present situation. Be glorified through the answer to my prayers. In Jesus' name. Amen.*

Notes

1. Barbara Wentroble, *Prophetic Intercession* (Ventura, CA: Renew Books, 1999), p. 97.
2. Chuck Pierce and Rebecca Wagner Sytsema, *The Future War of the Church* (Ventura, CA: Renew Books, 2001), pp. 75-76.
3. *Thepresidentialprayerteam.org* (accessed October 28, 2002).

CHAPTER 10

DECREES, DECLARATIONS AND PROCLAMATIONS

The world was still reeling from the September 11, 2001, terrorist attacks. Only a few weeks had passed since the Twin Towers had fallen, yet intercessors and leaders from more than 60 nations were gathering in Europe. Boarding an airplane was almost surreal, but I had to go. About 4,000 of us convened in Hanover, Germany. We were there to seek the Lord's strategy for releasing revival in the unevangelized area that extends from Iceland through Europe into Central Asia (often called the 40/70 window).

During one of the conference sessions, C. Peter Wagner stood and released a proclamation: "Foot-and-mouth disease is over." What a bold statement! Circumstances did not look as if the deadly disease had ended. Newspapers continued to report the devastating results on both the cattle owners and the economy. The media was still reporting on the spread and effects of the disease in various aspects of life. In fact, when we had arrived at the airport in Hanover, we had been required to walk across a floor mat that had been soaked in a chemical solution designed to prevent passengers from bringing the disease into the country.

One month later, however, the media announced that foot-and-mouth disease had ended. This was a manifestation on Earth of the words Peter Wagner had spoken into the atmosphere in Germany.

How did this happen? Probably a lot of skeptics would try to explain that this had occurred through natural means. Intercessors and spiritually astute people have no difficulty understanding what happened. Speaking forth God's intended will for Earth carries great power to perform His intended purpose. Words of authority, spoken in faith and boldness, release things that are in the Father's heart but are not yet visible on Earth. Believers have the authority to *create* God's will on Earth through words of proclamation and decrees that *cause* God's already existing will to be released.

APOSTOLIC FUNCTION

A proclamation is "something that is proclaimed or announced officially."[1] A declaration is similar: "a formal statement; proclamation."[2] A decree is "an official order, edict, or decision, as of a church, government, court, etc."[3] As ambassadors of the King of kings, we make official announcements, or edicts, to principalities and powers as well as to the inhabitants of Earth. Peter Wagner wrote about issuing declarations and proclamations in his book *Spheres of Authority*:

> James had full apostolic authority in the Jerusalem Council. After the apostles who were in attendance had said what they felt they needed to say about the issue of Gentile circumcision, James did not take a vote or form a commission to study the matter further or convene an executive council. He issued an apostolic declaration: "Therefore, I judge that we should not trouble those from among the Gentiles who are turning to God" (Acts 15:19). Notice the use of the first person singular in his statement. This is an apostle doing what an apostle is supposed to do.
>
> Notice also the response of the other, quite renowned, apostles who were present. They gladly received the authoritative word from James. "It pleased the apostles and the elders and the whole church" (Acts 15:22).[4]

Not all believers are apostles. However, we must be apostolic in our function as the Lord's ambassadors and intercessors. In my book *A People of Destiny*, I wrote about the authority released through powerful intercessors declaring and proclaiming the will of God:

> Not only do New Order people love to pray, they sense an authority in their prayers. They have an understanding from Scripture that they are God's representatives on Earth. As His representatives, they speak as with His voice. Prophetic intercession, proclamations, declarations, and prophetic songs are an integral part of the prayer life.

Recently I was part of a team of ministers speaking at a conference in Waco, Texas. The conference theme was "Seize the City." Intercessors gathered for several days to hear how they could bring their city under the lordship of Jesus. On one of the prayerwalks to historically strategic sites, we crossed a bridge over a river. About halfway across the bridge, an intercessor faced the city and cried out loudly, "Waco, hear the word of the Lord!" She then made prophetic proclamations about the will of the Lord for that city. The other intercessors verbally agreed by shouting, "Yes! Amen! Do it, Lord!" A sense that the proclamations were not merely the words of a human came upon the team. God had spoken prophetically through one of his representatives.[5]

Government officials sometimes release proclamations and decrees. Robert Winningham, Mayor of Downey, California, issued a written proclamation for Transformation Values Week, September 16-22, 2002:

City of Downey—Proclamation: Transformation Values Week

WHEREAS, for many years, pastors, churches, business people and political leaders in the city of Downey have worked together to bring about a time when citizens of all races, creeds and religions could agree on American traditional values; and;

WHEREAS, a voluntary committee of concerned Downey citizens have joined together to proclaim political, economic, cultural and spiritual values for our citizens to live, exhort, encourage and believe; and

WHEREAS, the community of Downey is invited to participate in a "March for Transformation by Traditional Values" on Saturday, September 8 and a community prayer service on Friday, September 14;

NOW, therefore I, Robert C. Winningham, Mayor of the city of Downey, do hereby proclaim September 10-16 be designated as a week to live, proclaim and to encourage the transformation of our traditional American values for betterment of Downey's political, educational, economic, cultural and spiritual growth.

Psalm 133:1 "How good and pleasant it is when brothers live together in unity."

> Signed,
> Robert C. Winningham
> Mayor[6]

WEAPONS OF WARFARE

Godly proclamations and declarations are not just words spoken into the air or written on a piece of paper. They are used to stop the evil purposes of the enemy and to release the blessings of God. Proclamations, declarations and decrees are weapons of warfare designed by the Lord to destroy onslaughts of wicked spirits:

> For though we walk in the flesh, we do not war according to the flesh, for the weapons of our warfare are not of the flesh, but divinely powerful for the destruction of fortresses (2 Cor. 10:3-4).

Julia Colgate spent nine years living in Southeast Asia. In the book *Longing to Call Them Sisters*, she wrote of dealing with occult activity among the Muslim women where she lived. Julia dealt with the demonic powers holding a family in fear and under a demonic curse:

> Several months ago, I was interceding for the hillside community where I live. My husband and I had just ministered to a young family and had seen the power of God at work freeing the young man from a curse brought into the home through a magic ring. As I prayed, I was filled with zeal as I proclaimed the Lord's holiness and power over the young family's home and the surrounding neighborhood. Suddenly, I realized God was leading me to renounce the power of amulets held by all my neighbors. I prayed that the amulets would be cut off from their source and dry up and become useless and that my neighbors would become disillusioned with them.[7]

Julia went on to say that even though her faith was strong that day, she did not see any results for four months. Several months later, however, while visiting with some of her neighbors, one lady shared how she was discouraged about the results of some of the amulets in her home. The neighbor even used scissors to destroy some of his magic belts made with amulets. Julia was able to confirm that no good results had come from the amulets since she had prayed. The neighbor was shifting her allegiance from fear of the demonic to the fear of God! God used the weapon of proclamation to turn the neighbor's heart away from the enemy's deception.

Authority for All Believers

- Who is able to make such powerful decrees and proclamations?

- Is this only for those who are ordained as ministers?
- Is this authority reserved for veteran world-class intercessors?
- Are those young in intercession able to operate in this type of authority?

The Bible reveals an authority that God has purposed for all believers. Paul encourages the believers at the church at Ephesus to understand the grace given to them. He had received a revelation from the Lord concerning the power of God that would be demonstrated by the Church against principalities and powers:

> To me, the very least of all saints, this grace was given, to preach to the Gentiles the unfathomable riches of Christ, and to bring to light what is the administration of the mystery which for ages has been hidden in God who created all things; so that the manifold wisdom of God might now be made known through the church to the rulers and the authorities in the heavenly places. This was in accordance with the eternal purpose which He carried out in Christ Jesus our Lord, in whom we have boldness and confident access through faith in Him. . . . Now to Him who is able to do far more abundantly beyond all that we ask or think, according to the power that works within us (Eph. 3:8-20).

Third-Day people speak words of power and authority as they decree the will of God.

Just as the Early Church did, the Third-Day Church will demonstrate to the evil principalities and powers the authority to cause God's will to be manifest on Earth. Third-Day people speak words of power and authority as they decree the will of God. No longer do we simply receive and accept whatever happens, because not everything that happens is the will of God. Children are being used for pornography, women are being physically abused, sickness and disease are destroying lives—such situations are not God's will! The Church is called to arise in this hour and exert authority in intercession for such situations to change.

Discerning and Declaring God's Will

My friend Dutch Sheets has operated powerfully in the last several years to unite intercessors for a change in the government of the United States. After seeking the will of God, he alerts intercessors and leaders to pray in unity for God's will in the civil government of our nation.

During the presidential election of 2000, Dutch made a trip to Washington, D.C. After many confirmations that he knew the will of God for the office of president, Dutch released declarations into the atmosphere surrounding the White House. He was not doing this as a Republican or a Democrat. He was doing this as a prophetic proclamation for the will of God to be accomplished. He wrote about this bold act of prayer in the book *Destiny of a Nation*:

> We first prayed for then Vice President Al Gore and his family. We blessed him in numerous ways and asked God to fulfill the destiny He had designed for him. We then, however, spoke out, took the authority of the keys, and spiritually closed the door of the White House to him, decreeing that he would not enter there to lead this nation.

We then proceeded to decree that the door to the White House was open to George W. Bush, and that he would enter it as the president of the United States. This intense prayer time lasted about 30 minutes.

Presumptuous? Arrogant? Some would no doubt feel that it was. However, by that time I was thoroughly convinced God had confirmed again and again that we had this authority in the spirit and that we were to exercise it. I was willing to obey God even if it might look foolish to others. Agreeing with the prayers of millions of people that presumably by then had been stored in the heavenly prayer bowls mentioned in Revelation 5, we simply made the declarations that turned out to be the final release. A few days later, the Supreme Court made its decisive ruling and Vice President Gore conceded.[8]

How were Dutch Sheets and other intercessors able to know God's will, so they could release those powerful declarations? They first had to discern the will of God. In the Old Testament the high priest wore an ephod that had an opening. Inside the breastplate of the ephod were two objects: the Urim and Thummim. No one knows for certain what these objects were. Some translators believe these words mean "lights" and "perfections." Whenever the high priest needed the wisdom of God, he would use these objects to somehow reveal God's will or judgment.

Using the translations of "lights" and "perfections" for "Urim" and "Thummim," I like to think the lights signify revelation by the Spirit of God, while perfections represent the Word of God. Whenever we need to know God's will, we can discern it through the Word and the Spirit. Dutch and the other intercessors understood the Scriptures concerning God's desire for righteousness in a nation. They also discerned by the Spirit that the Lord wanted to use George W. Bush to turn this nation toward righteousness. God does not hate Al Gore; He simply wanted to use someone else for that season.

We have the Word of God—the Bible—and the Spirit of God within us to help us discern God's will in various situations. Every believer has access to the wisdom of God through these means.

POWERFUL RESULTS

The results of proclamations and decrees are powerful. The first result is that evil powers are rendered powerless. I wrote about this aspect of intercession in my book *Prophetic Intercession*:

> Proclamation carries with it a nature of binding, commanding and settling. The word "bind" means "to fasten or to tie up with chains or a cord." Prophetic proclamations released through the mouths of intercessors have the ability to tie up the effect of evil powers like an animal tied with chains or a cord.[9]

The second result of proclamations and decrees is that faith is released to the hearers of the proclamation or decree:

> So faith comes from hearing, and hearing by the word of Christ (Rom. 10:17).

The words of authority in the proclamation or decree cause those who hear to come into agreement with the words spoken. Even the person speaking the proclamation or decree steps into a higher level of faith!

Another result of the use of proclamations is that God's will and blessings are released on Earth. We are admonished in the

Bible to give God no rest until His word and will are manifest on Earth:

> On your walls, O Jerusalem, I have appointed watchmen; all day and all night they will never keep silent. You who remind the LORD, take no rest for yourselves; and give Him no rest until He establishes and makes Jerusalem a praise in the earth (Isa. 62:6-7).

As watchmen intercessors, we are not to keep silent. We are to continue to release God's word and will until He establishes our families, cities and territories as a praise in all the earth!

Throughout the Bible we understand the powerful results of people who persevered until there were positive manifestations for their assignments. Esther refused to give up until the enemy was destroyed. The king loved Esther and issued an edict, or decree, for the destruction of the enemies of God's people. As a result of that decree, God's covenant people gained the victory over their enemies:

> Now in the twelfth month (that is, the month Adar), on the thirteenth day when the king's command and edict were about to be executed, on the day when the enemies of the Jews hoped to gain the mastery over them, it was turned to the contrary so that the Jews themselves gained the mastery over those who hated them (Esther 9:1).

Intercessors, today refuse to stop declaring with authority the word and the will of God until it manifests itself on Earth. Ask the Lord to fill your mouth with His word and His will. Then release those words with great expectancy. Declare that the works of evil spirits are bound. Call forth the will of God into your situation!

Heavenly Father, thank You that I can know Your will. You have given me Your Word and Your Spirit. You have also given me the authority to declare Your will on Earth. With that understanding, I open my mouth and release proclamations of victory for Your Church. I release words that bind the works of darkness. I call forth Your will to be released on Earth. I declare that You reign today. I will give You no rest until my family and my area are a praise to You in all the earth. With Your keys of authority I now lock up the powers of darkness. With those keys, I also open the door for Your will to manifest itself. Thank You in advance for the manifestation that You have heard this prayer. In the name of Jesus I pray. Amen.

Notes

1. *Webster's New World College Dictionary,* 4th ed., s.v " proclamation."
2. Ibid, s.v. "declaration."
3. Ibid. s.v. "decree."
4. C. Peter Wagner, *Spheres of Authority* (Colorado Springs, CO: Wagner Publications, 2002), pp. 75-76.
5. Barbara Wentroble, *A People of Destiny* (Colorado Springs, CO: Wagner Publications, 2000), p. 46.
6. Public domain.
7. Julia Colgate, quoted in Fran Love and Jeleta Eckheart, eds., *Longing to Call Them Sisters* (Pasadena, CA: William Carey Library, 2000), p. 47.
8. C. Peter Wagner, ed., *Destiny of a Nation* (Colorado Springs, CO: Wagner Publications, 2001), pp. 83-84.
9. Barbara Wentroble, *Prophetic Intercession* (Ventura, CA: Renew Books, 1999), p. 101.

CHAPTER 11

ANGELS

Angels are a popular subject today. Movies and TV programs often portray various types of angels. Some look like cherubs with wings and white clothing. Others look like ordinary people who do extraordinary tasks. Most people I know have seen very few, if any, angels in real life. Others tell of frequent visitations by angels. I have had only a couple of actual glances at what I believe were angels, yet I have witnessed the activities of angels on many occasions.

ENCOUNTERING ANGELS

Sometimes we can encounter angels without recognizing them at the moment, as expressed in Hebrews 13:2: "Do not neglect to show hospitality to strangers, for by this some have entertained angels without knowing it." Often my family and I have wondered if we once encountered an angel without recognizing him.

The incident took place right after we had delivered a missionary family to Guadalajara, Mexico. Only our family was in the car, and we were thankful to be nearing the United States border, since none of us spoke Spanish. We drove late into the night, so we could get across the border and be able to communicate in English before stopping for the night at a motel.

We were only about 25 miles from the border when suddenly we heard a loud noise. My husband, Dale, pulled the car to the side of the road and stopped, as our hope for familiar territory faded fast. We soon discovered that one of the tires had gone flat. We were stranded in the middle of the night with three small children. No town was in sight. On top of that, our flashlight did not work. However, Dale worked in the dark to exchange the flat tire with the spare. While making the change, one of the bolts used to hold the tire on the car fell from his hand. The ground was covered with gravel, and with no light, we could not see to find the bolt. All three of the children began crawling around and feeling the ground, hoping to locate the missing part. Dale prayed, "Lord, help us find that bolt." After several fear-filled minutes, his prayer was answered. Now we could get on our way—or so we thought.

After mounting the spare tire, we discovered that it was flat as well. Dale then stood beside the road and prayed that the Lord would send someone to help us. Although we had not seen any traffic up to this time, it was only a couple of minutes before a large truck came over the hill. After seeing Dale waving at him, the driver pulled his vehicle to where we were stranded, and Dale showed him our flat. Although the driver did not speak English, he quickly recognized our problem.

The driver unrolled a hose attached to an air pump on his truck. It extended just far enough to reach the rear tire on our car. How unusual that the driver would have an air pump with a long hose! Most truck drivers do not.

The driver put air in the tire and checked to be sure that it was adequately inflated. When Dale tried to express thanks and offer him money for his service, the man refused. While we drove the car back on the highway, the man followed us in his truck all the way to the border, obviously wanting to be sure we were able to make it across safely.

Ministering Spirits

Who was this man? We have often asked ourselves this question. Did the Lord, in answer to Dale's prayer, send an angel? We believe so, though we will probably never know for certain until we get to heaven. However, angel or not, that man fulfilled one of the assignments of angels, which is to help believers in times of need:

> Are [angels] not all ministering spirits, sent out to render service for the sake of those who will inherit salvation? (Heb. 1:14).

The word "angel" in the Greek language is *aggelos*, which means "a messenger."[1] There are times when an angel brings a message from God. God, on occasion, gives a person the ability to see into the unseen world. When this occurs, the individual is able physically to see angels.

God, on occasion, gives a person the ability to see into the unseen world.

We cannot be certain when God created the angels. However, we can make a reasonable guess that they were formed just prior to the creation of Earth because Genesis 1:1 records that heaven and Earth were created in that order: heaven first and then Earth. Since heaven is a model for Earth, we can assume the angels were created first, along with heaven. After the creation of heaven and the heavenly host, God created the earth and mankind.

Throughout the Bible we find stories of people who saw angels. The prophet Ezekiel looked up and saw a cloud and, within the cloud, angels (see Ezek. 1). An angel spoke to Philip and brought him directions from God (see Acts 8:26). The Lord sent an angel to kill Herod (see Acts 12:23). An angel visited and encouraged Paul, assuring him that God would preserve his life and the lives of the entire crew (see Acts 27:23-24). John received the message of the Lord from an angel (see Rev. 1:1). Numerous other examples of angels involved with and ministering to humans can be found in the Bible.

Functions of Angels

Modern man often denies the existence and operation of angels on Earth. Many today believe, like the deists, that God created the universe billions of years ago. They also believe that He wound the world up like a clock and then left it to run itself. The doctrine of deism is that God created the world and its natural laws but refrains from intervening in history with miracles or making any alteration to the natural order.

The Bible does not teach this concept. It teaches that *God is intimately involved in running the universe all the time.* Miracles happen when the Lord does something different from the way He ordinarily does it. Miracles merely operate by God's law, which is His Word:

[God] works all things after the counsel of His will (Eph. 1:11).

Although God is intimately involved in running the universe at all times, He sometimes uses angels to assist in the running of the world. These angels are perfect servants to God; therefore, they are models for us to follow as God's servants on Earth. Since angels are an example for us, we need to understand some of their functions.

Obeying God's Will

Obeying the will of God is the main function of angelic beings. Lucifer and all other angels at one time dwelt in heaven. They fully obeyed the Lord's will. At some point Lucifer led a rebellion, and all the angels were tested in their loyalty to God. The Bible says that one-third of the angels chose to follow in Lucifer's rebellion and were subsequently cast out of heaven and into the earthly realm (see Isa. 14:4-23; Ezek. 28:1-19).

The result was a war between two kingdoms—the kingdom of God (light) and the kingdom of Satan (darkness). Angels of God serve and obey Him. Fallen angels, or evil spirits, serve Satan and do his will. Evil angels are authentic, and intercessors need to understand their operation. Though space does not permit an in-depth teaching on this subject, it is important for intercessors to access a spiritual weapon the Lord makes available for believers. This weapon, as we saw earlier in Hebrews 1:14, is His angels: "Are they not all ministering spirits, sent out to render service for the sake of those who will inherit salvation?" My purpose in this chapter is to emphasize the help available from God's angels to all believers.

Angels obey the will of God at all times. However, they do not obey God's will merely because they *know* His will. It seems that sometimes angels need *words spoken* for them to obey. In January 2002, I was attending the annual meeting of the Apostolic Council of Prophetic Elders in Colorado Springs, Colorado. Approximately 20 prophets from the United States and several more from other countries attended this meeting.

During one of the sessions we were praying and asking the Lord to give us strategy and show us how to reach the people in

Cuba. A prophet from Germany had his eyes open and saw angels in the room as we prayed. He described the angels as being exceptionally large and shuffling their feet back and forth as if anxious to get going on an assignment. When the description of the angels was given to the group, someone asked the question, "What are they waiting for?" The answer came quickly: "They are waiting to be released." The group, joined in unity, shouted as one voice, "Go and fulfill the will of the Lord."

After we sensed the angels had left the room, the same prophet gave us another picture. "The angels left something," he noticed.

"What did they leave?" we asked.

"They left two pots of gold," he answered.

"Why did they leave gold?" one person inquired. When the answer was not immediately forthcoming, we began to pray and ask the Lord why the angels had left the gold.

After several minutes of praying, various prophets in the room gave pieces of the answer to the question. The conclusion was that God is transferring wealth into the hands of His people. Even though there have been numerous prophecies of this in the past, it has not happened until now. The reason it has not happened before is because the Church would have spent the wealth on herself. God is transferring wealth into the hands of a compassionate Church that will feed the poor and care for the needy. The angels left gold for those who would obey the will of God and care for those in need.

Although the will of God was for the angels to go and fulfill His will on Earth, it seems that they waited for words to be spoken. Apparently, words in the mouths of believers release angels to fulfill their assignments. I do not make a practice of commanding angels to obey; I do make a practice of asking the Lord to release His angels for the task needed at the moment. These supernatural spirits are released to do the will of God when we ask the Lord for their assistance.

Several years ago I was ministering deliverance to a man who had come out of occult involvement. A couple of other people were in the room. Suddenly the man we were ministering to tried to jump out of his chair and run. "Lord, cause Your angels to hold him," I cried. Immediately, the man's feet were crossed and appeared to lock in place. He sat back down and did not try to get up until the session was over.

At the end of the ministry session, he attempted to stand but could not get his feet out of the crossed and locked position. Not understanding what had happened to him, he began to panic. Suddenly I remembered that we had not

> *Words in the mouths of believers release angels to fulfill their assignments.*

asked the angels to let the man go. "Lord, have the angels turn him loose," I prayed. Instantly the man's feet relaxed, and he straightened them, so he could stand. The angels responded to spoken words and obeyed the will of God.

Powerful Beings

So often angels are pictured as sweet cherubs playing softly on harps, but angels are not wimpy little creatures. They are powerful beings able to wage a mighty battle and secure the victory:

> Bless the LORD, you His angels, mighty in strength, who perform His word, obeying the voice of His word! Bless the LORD, all you His hosts, you who serve Him, doing His will   (Ps. 103:20-21).

These strong angels respond when they hear the words spoken by God's people, declaring His mind and will for Earth. They then go forth in great power and obedience.

Often I have seen the results of the strength of angels during times of ministry. A person being set free from demonic activity will sometimes attempt to hit or throw something at the person ministering to him or her. When that happens to me, I call for angelic help by praying, "Lord, release Your angels to hold!" Immediately the person's arms will lock in place or his or her body becomes immovable. The strong angels hold the person until the ministry is completed.

Assistance in Warfare

Another function of angels is that they are used for assistance in warfare. Angels do not do what we have been assigned to do, yet they are our assistants in warfare. Daniel 9 records the story of the angel Gabriel, who brought understanding and insight to Daniel concerning the future war of God's people. Daniel had persevered in prayer. As a result, angelic activity was released in heaven. One day a powerful angel appeared to Daniel and brought him understanding of the battle:

> Now while I was speaking and praying, and confessing my sin and the sin of my people Israel, and presenting my supplication before the LORD my God in behalf of the holy mountain of my God, while I was still speaking in prayer, then the man Gabriel, whom I had seen in the vision previously, came to me in my extreme weariness about the time of the evening offering. He gave me instruction and talked with me and said, "O Daniel, I have now come forth to give you insight with under-standing. At the beginning of your supplications the command was issued, and I have come to tell you, for you are highly esteemed; so give heed to the message and gain understanding of the vision" (vv. 20-23).

Daniel's prayer released great power and an authority to gain understanding and to govern in the heavens. These words caused the heavenly host to engage in powerful battle against the evil spirits that sought to hinder the release of God's will. The Lord's powerful Church is arising today, assisted by angels for great victories in the days ahead.

When the time came for the Israelites to be released from Egypt, they were required to put the blood of the *Pascal* (Passover) lamb on the doorposts of their houses (see Exod. 12:7). When the death angel came by, he would not destroy the firstborn of those who had the blood on their doors (see v. 23). As a result of the devastation by the death angel upon the Egyptians, they cried out for the Israelites to leave Egypt. Not only that, but they also provided silver, gold and clothing for the people (see vv. 33-36). The death angel was used in warfare to bring release to the Israelite captives. The Lord today is setting entire territories and nations free from the captivity of the enemy. He is transferring wealth from the hands of the wicked to a righteous people who advance His purposes on Earth (see Prov. 13:22).

Protection from Backlash

After the initial victory in Egypt, the enemy sought to bring backlash to God's people. In this situation, the enemy was attempting to attack once again after Israel's victory in Egypt. I wrote about this aspect of warfare in my book *Prophetic Intercession*:

> The enemy does not stop his maneuvers to interfere with the will of God just because we have experienced a victory. He is stubborn in his pursuit to stop the plan of God. Therefore, he engages in an activity often referred to as backlash. One of Webster's definitions for "backlash" is "a quick, sharp recoil."

Considering the fact that the enemy is likened to a serpent or snake, we can understand this definition. A serpent will recoil and try to strike a target he considers as his enemy. Satan does the same thing in spiritual warfare. Many times in spiritual battle, he will recoil and try to strike again after God's people have secured a victory.[2]

After the Israelites left Egypt, the pharaoh's army pursued them. The demonic ruler had changed his mind about letting God's people go. However, help was available! The angel of God and the pillar of cloud moved from the front of the Israelites and stood behind them (see Exod. 14:19-20). Israel experienced light, while the Egyptians had darkness.

For He will give His angels charge concerning you, to guard you in all your ways (Ps. 91:11).

God used the angel to provide protection against the enemy's backlash and to bring his people to another victory.

Discerning of Spirits
The ability of man to see angels is called "the distinguishing [or discerning] of spirits" and is one of the gifts of the Holy Spirit (1 Cor. 12:7-11). Discerning of spirits is the divine ability to see the presence and activity of a spirit, whether good or bad.

We believe our granddaughter Lindsey recently saw a good angel. She had wakened from a nap, and her mother, Michelle, was changing her diaper.

"Angel," Lindsey announced as she pointed to a corner in the ceiling of her room.

"Did you see an angel?" her mother asked.

"Angel," Lindsey repeated. Then, covering her eyes, she said, "Bright!"

Although Lindsey's parents had read her a couple of stories that included angels, they had never actually talked to her about the subject. That day, however, Lindsey kept pointing to the same spot on the ceiling and saying, "Angel. Bright. Candle." She understood that candles are bright. Due to the fact that she was only two years old at the time, we are not sure if she actually saw a candle or if it was just her way of expressing the brightness of the angel. Nevertheless, she was intent on conveying the presence of a very bright angel at the top of her room.

The Lord sometimes gives us an ability to see the unseen. However, it really is not as important to see angels as it is to know that they are available to us as believers:

> The angel of the LORD encamps around those who fear Him, and rescues them (Ps. 34:7).

Angels function outside Earth's limitation in order to bring God's people to the victory of the battle. Intercessors have myriad angels available to assist them in spiritual warfare. Ask the Lord to release angels to assist you in gaining the victory.

> *Heavenly Father, thank You for providing help in times of battle. I acknowledge Your wisdom in releasing angels that are assigned to me for protection during these battles. I ask You to open my spiritual eyes to see and discern the help You make available to me. I will not fear the enemy but will walk in the fear of the Lord. You have released angels of great strength to equip me for victory. Thank You that I will see the result of angelic activity on Earth, even as it is in heaven. In Jesus' powerful name. Amen.*

Notes

1. James Strong, *The Exhaustive Concordance of the Bible: Greek Dictionary of the New Testament* (McLean, VA: MacDonald Publishing Company, n.d.), p. 7.
2. Barbara Wentroble, *Prophetic Intercession* (Ventura, CA: Renew Books, 1999), p. 170.

CHAPTER 12

THE HARVEST

I love to read stories of past revivals. These stories usually include keys that help us know how to release revival in our generation. A major key to revival has always been a movement of prayer. Dr. A. T. Pierson once said, "There has never been a spiritual awakening in any country or locality that did not begin in united prayer."[1]

One of the major revivals in history was the Welsh revival. Sustained, united, fervent prayer was a major key in releasing the revival that brought a mighty harvest of souls and social transformation to the country of Wales. Dr. J. Edwin Orr, a prominent scholar of revivals, wrote detailed books about evangelical awakenings. In one of his messages, he described the harvest resulting from a powerful movement of prayer for revival:

> The social impact was astounding. For example, judges were presented with white gloves, not a case to try; no

robberies, no burglaries, no rapes, no murders, and no embezzlements, nothing. District councils held emergency meetings to discuss what to do with the police now that they are unemployed.

In one place the sergeant of police was sent for and asked, "What do you do with your time?" He replied, "Before the revival, we had two main jobs, to prevent crime and to control crowds, as at football games. Since the revival started there is practically no crime. So we just go with the crowds."

A councilor asked, "What does that mean?" The sergeant replied, "You know where the crowds are. They are packing out the churches." "But how does that affect the police?" He was told, "We have seventeen police in our station, but we have quartets, and if any church wants a quartet to sing, they simply call the police station."

As the revival swept Wales, drunkenness was cut in half. There was a wave of bankruptcies, but nearly all taverns. There was even a slowdown in the mines, for so many Welsh coal miners were converted and stopped using bad language that the horses that dragged the coal trucks in the mines could not understand what was being said to them.

That revival also affected sexual moral standards. I had discovered through the figures given by British government experts that in Radnorshire and Merionethshire the illegitimate birth rate had dropped 44% within a year of the beginning of the revival.[2]

God's Vehicle for Transformation

Nations today, including our own, need to experience God's presence in a new way. The media constantly reports the increase in crime, poverty, immorality and lawlessness found in every segment of society. Reading the newspaper or listening to the TV news reminds us of the people in Noah's day:

> Then the LORD saw that the wickedness of man was great on the earth, and that every intent of the thoughts of his heart was only evil continually (Gen. 6:5).

The purpose of authority in intercession is to release the harvest, which is the will of God, on Earth. The Church is God's vehicle for transformation on Earth. A government program will never bring the needed change. Social programs only put bandages on the problems. Only the power of the Holy Spirit can change the hearts and minds of mankind. Bringing the Holy Spirit to those in need is the responsibility of the Church. Yet the Church has not fully awakened to her God-given mandate (see Gen. 1:26-28). Religion has kept the Church focusing on leaving Earth and enjoying the benefits of heaven. Although we rightly long for heaven, it is time to redirect our focus. That is why Jesus taught His disciples to pray about change coming to the earth rather than praying about escaping and going to heaven:

The purpose of authority in intercession is to release the harvest.

> Your kingdom come. Your will be done, on earth as it is in heaven (Matt. 6:10).

God has intercessors today who have awakened from their slumber and entered a season of powerful, authoritative prayer for the release of the harvest. Although we have seen prayer movements throughout history, we have now entered a period of intercession unlike any previous time!

CURRENT WORLDWIDE PRAYER MOVEMENT

I have enjoyed the privilege of connecting with intercessors from around the world since the early 1990s. Peter Wagner has been a powerful instrument in bringing this prayer movement to a new level. The movement has spread like wildfire throughout the nations of the world. I love what Peter said about this incredible period of intercession:

> The current worldwide prayer movement is out of control! It is, of course, under the sovereign control of the Holy Spirit, but no human being or human institution or human-operated computer bank could possibly keep track of a spontaneous movement of such magnitude. Its dimensions are awesome—unprecedented in the history of Christianity.[3]

God has a harvest of souls that are ready throughout the world. It is His desire that they know Him. For His will for the harvest to be brought into the Kingdom, believers must cry out in prayer. That is exactly what is happening in China, as revival, brought about by the prayers of faithful intercessors, sweeps the land. The following is an excerpt of a report I recently read from a group of intercessors in the Henan province of China:

> It is pitch dark and the temperature is below zero. There are about seventy of us. Your body would welcome sleep in a warm blanket, but you are excited by the prospect of being with God. First we sing choruses of love for Him,

love for one another, and the vision to reach the nation for God. Then come words of knowledge; there has been bad feelings between members of the group and God will not move unless there is reconciliation. Everyone is in tears; all are hugging each other and confessing their coldness of heart. This goes on for two hours.

Then comes a prophecy: "It is time to take the land. Be strong and bold, for I will build My Church. Make war on the powers of darkness. Call on Me and ask for the heathen." Some dance and clap their hands, others are prostrate in humility before God. Then all rise, hands lifted and joined together, and begin to engage their foe. This is not petition, it is proclamation. They know God will do it. . . .

The prayer rolls down the mountain like an avalanche. Soon, it is 4:30 and you have to return—for the daily prayer meeting at 5:30 A.M.[4]

INTERCESSION IN THE WORKPLACE

Intercessors not only meet in churches to pray, but they also meet in workplaces to pray. Business people are recognizing that they have a call on their lives. They have been called to the workplace not simply to receive a paycheck; they are there to bring salvation to the lost and transformation to their spheres of influence.

Tiffany Ramsey is one of those who have a heart to see a harvest of souls reaped at her place of employment. I wrote about her in my book *A People of Destiny*:

Tiffany went to her supervisor and asked for the use of a meeting room for the lunch hour one day each week. Since Tiffany is an excellent employee and the favor of God is on her, she was given permission. People in her workplace began attending the weekly Bible studies. They have been receiving Jesus as their Savior, filled with the Holy Spirit, and experiencing healing and deliverance. The Bible study is now a company recognized Employee Special Interest Group entitled "Ambassadors for Christ."[5]

Prayer in the workplace is not new to our generation. In 1857 a man by the name of Jeremiah Lanphier began holding prayer meetings at noon each day in New York City. An interesting point about these prayer meetings is that they were held in a church near the location of the former World Trade Center, which was destroyed by terrorists on September 11, 2001.

Jeremiah was a middle-aged businessman with no wife or children. Although he was busy working in the slums of Hell's Kitchen, holding Bible studies and distributing tracts, he saw little fruit from his efforts. He became tired, discouraged and weak from his efforts to reach the lost. Finally he asked permission to use a room at the Old Dutch Church North, so he could cry out to God for spiritual strength.

Jeremiah invited other businessmen to join him for prayer during their lunch hour. On the first day, he prayed alone for the first 30 minutes; then six other men showed up. Two weeks later over 40 people came to pray. It was only a matter of time before other churches and meeting halls were filled with people praying. Tens of thousands of people in New York were meeting regularly for prayer. As a result, over 150,000 people became believers.

GOD'S CALL AND OUR RESPONSE

Jeremiah Lanphier's prayer meetings released a revival throughout America and abroad. God has promised revival and the healing of a nation when His people pray:

[If] My people who are called by My name humble themselves and pray and seek My face and turn from their wicked ways, then I will hear from heaven, will forgive their sin and will heal their land (2 Chron. 7:14).

Today people are acknowledging God's direction to meet together to humble themselves and pray in homes, churches and workplaces, seeking his healing, blessing and revival in the land.

Jesus was filled with mercy and compassion when He looked at the multitudes in need of God's love and power. He instructed His disciples to pray for laborers to help bring in the harvest:

Then He said to His disciples, "The harvest is plentiful, but the workers are few. Therefore beseech the Lord of the harvest to send out workers into His harvest" (Matt. 9:37-38).

FINISH THE LORD'S WORK

What, then, should our response be to this God-orchestrated call to prayer? First, we should have a passionate desire to finish the work the Lord has for us. Too many people start well, but they do not finish well. History records the lives of great men and women with incredible giftings and potential, many of whom started their assignments in powerful ways. Along the way, however, some lost the zeal of their first love. Jesus commended the church at Ephesus and then spoke this warning through the apostle John:

But I have this against you, that you have left your first love (Rev. 2:4).

The Lord has given each of us a goal and purpose for our lives. We have Jesus as an example to follow in reaching that goal and fulfilling that purpose:

> Jesus said to them, "My food is to do the will of Him who sent Me and to accomplish His work" (John 4:34).

The word "accomplish" means "to complete; finish; to reach one's prescribed goal."[6] Jesus was saying in the above Scripture that the thing (food) that propelled Him on was to reach God's goal and fulfill God's purpose. Later, in His high priestly prayer recorded in John 17, Jesus declared that He had done just that:

> I glorified You on the earth, having accomplished the work which You have given Me to do (v. 4).

Our nourishment and strength should come from a deep commitment to finish the goal and fulfill the purpose the Lord has set before us.

A New Mind-Set

A new mind-set is necessary for us to reach our God-given goal, or purpose. In other words, our thinking must change. An understanding of synergy will help strengthen our commitment and aid in our comprehension.

When we pray, our prayers are added to the prayers of previous generations. As we join our prayers to prayers that have gone before us, the power of these prayers is not just added, but it also multiplies exponentially!

> How could one chase a thousand, and two put ten thousand to flight? (Deut. 32:30).

Our prayer then becomes the mighty weight of many generations. Therefore, quitting is not an option!

Sent Ones

The next response should be to recognize that we are "sent ones." In our day, God is raising up a people with an understanding of being sent into the world to do the will of the Father: "As You sent Me into the world, I also have sent them into the world" (John 17:18). I wrote about sent ones in my book *A People of Destiny*:

> They are willing to follow the leading of the Lord into uncharted waters. They have a desire to be positioned in the place where the Lord can use them to help bring forth a great harvest. Therefore, they allow the Lord to position them as instruments of harvest for His kingdom purposes. . . .
>
> The new positioning involves moving from a "lay person" mentality to a "minister" mentality. That means you must be able to see the harvest field in the place God has chosen for you. The harvest field may be at the grocery store. It may be at the bank, office, gas station, your child's soccer practice, or in your neighborhood. The harvest field is wherever you are. You are not there for the obvious reasons. You are there because the Lord has positioned you in that place for His purposes.[7]

ADVANCING GOD'S KINGDOM

Another response should be a vision for advancing the kingdom of God in the world. Our assignment on Earth is not merely to breathe in and breathe out. We are sent as laborers in God's field. Our job assignment is to do our part in extending the kingdom of God into every sphere of life and society. Our prayers should be that the Lord uses us to impact Earth with the irresistible love and power of God. All other kingdoms of this world will fall, but we are part of an eternal kingdom that will never end:

> *Our assignment on Earth is not merely to breathe in and breathe out. We are sent as laborers in God's field.*

> In the days of those kings the God of heaven will set up a kingdom which will never be destroyed, and that kingdom will not be left for another people; it will crush and put an end to all these kingdoms, but it will itself endure forever (Dan. 2:44).

Great joy is our portion as we enter into this season of harvest. The apostle Paul prayed that we would see with the eyes of faith and know our inheritance. We are not limited to what our natural eyes see. God has seated us in the heavenlies with Christ Jesus (see Eph. 1:18-23). From that position we see from God's perspective. We can then delight in the answer to our prayers. The end result of our powerful, authoritative prayers is the harvest of multitudes that are destined to enter the kingdom of God:

> Ask of Me, and I will surely give the nations as Your inheritance, and the very ends of the earth as Your possession (Ps. 2:8).

STEWARDS OF GOD'S ESTATE

The Church is the steward of God's estate, which is Earth. We can be stewards of influence for either good or evil. God has given us a mandate to exercise dominion over His estate (see Gen. 1:26-28) and to prepare His people to respond to the presence of the Lord. We are involved in an important dimension of participation with the Lord in stewarding Earth. Alistair Petrie quotes the remarks of Douglas John Hall concerning the awesome responsibility we have as God's stewards:

> Although a steward of God (or Christ), like the stewards of earthly lords, can claim nothing for him or herself, that steward is not merely an outsider—hired help, so to speak. Rather the steward participates in the very "household of God." As such, the steward is "called" and "enabled" to share His grace (Eph. 3:8) with others, and to bring them in turn into God's household.[8]

Through authoritative prayer, we steward Earth by clearing the atmosphere of hindering spirits that seek to keep the eyes of the harvest blinded from seeing the truth (see 2 Cor. 4:4). We strip away the blinders, so people can find the path to their God-ordained destiny. We remove any rocks of stumbling or roots that hold back a plentiful harvest.

As we are faithful in prayer, the Lord will allow us to experience the delight of harvest. The Bible gives a beautiful picture of the Church in the book of Ruth. Ruth was faithful in the field of Boaz. Because of her faithfulness in small things, Boaz ordered his servants to purposefully leave extra portions of the harvest for Ruth:

> Also you shall purposely pull out for her some grain from the bundles and leave it that she may glean, and do not rebuke her (2:16).

Ruth experienced the joy and satisfaction of reaping an increase in the fruits of harvest. Our heavenly Boaz, Jesus, will cause us to participate in an increase of the fruits of harvest during this season of reaping.

I remember a song we sang years ago. One line was a prayer that those who come behind us would find us faithful. That is the cry of my heart. May the next generation rejoice in the mighty harvest that has resulted from a faithful army of intercessors who prayed in great authority for God's will to be done on Earth, even as it is in heaven!

Heavenly Father, I offer myself to be used as an instrument to bring revival to Earth. I ask You to grace me with the ability to finish the goal You have given me. With faith in my heart, I receive the revelation that when I pray, I am not merely offering up my own prayers to You; my prayers are joined with the prayers of previous generations. There is therefore great power in my prayers.

Thank You for sending me into the world to accomplish Your will. I now receive new vision for advancing Your kingdom wherever I go. It is with great joy and thanksgiving that I pray with a higher level of authority so that people who sit in darkness can see Your great light. Thank You that a new joy fills my heart as I offer my life to help bring in a mighty harvest for Your glory and for Your honor. Be glorified through my obedience to Your will. May history record the harvest resulting from the prayers of my generation of intercessors. In Jesus' name I pray. Amen!

Notes

1. J. Edwin Orr, "Revival and Prayer," *dunamai.com*. http://dunamai.com/articles/general/revival.htm (accessed November 3, 2002).
2. Ibid., (accessed January 21, 2003).
3. Michael Ebert, ed., *Window Watchman* (Colorado Springs, CO: Christian Information Network, 1994), p. 9.

4. "China: It's Time to Take the Land!" *Hong Kong and China Ministry Report*, *Jesus Army*. http://www.jesus.org.uk/china.html (accessed January 21, 2003).

5. Barbara Wentroble, *A People of Destiny* (Colorado Springs, CO: Wagner Publications, 2000), p. 40.

6. Spiros Zodhiates, *Hebrew-Greek Keyword Study Bible (New American Standard Version)* (Chattanooga, TN: AMG Publishers, 1990), p. 1880.

7. Wentroble, *A People of Destiny*, pp. 43-44.

8. Douglas John Hall, quoted in Alistair Petrie, *Releasing Heaven on Earth* (Grand Rapids, MI: Chosen Books, 2000), p. 237.